Scrum

The complete guide about Scrum -
Halve your working time by producing
twice as much

John Rich

Table of Contents

Preface

Scrum itself is a straightforward system for powerful group coordinated effort on complex items. Scrum co-makers Ken Schwaber and Jeff Sutherland have composed The Scrum Guide to clarify Scrum obviously and concisely. This Guide contains the meaning of Scrum. This definition comprises of Scrum's jobs, occasions, antiquities, and the guidelines that quandary them together.

Scrum is:

Lightweight

Easy to get it

Hard to ace

Scrum is straightforward. It is something contrary to a major assortment of interlaced required segments. Scrum isn't an approach. Scrum actualizes the logical technique for induction. Scrum replaces a customized algorithmic methodology with a heuristic one, with deference for individuals and self-association to manage unconventionality and taking care of complex issues. The beneath realistic speaks to Scrum in real life as depicted by Ken Schwaber and Jeff Sutherland in their book Software in 30 Days taking us from arranging through programming conveyance.

Scrum Values Although constantly viewed as a piece of Scrum and regularly expounded on, in July 2016, the Scrum Values were added to The Scrum Guide. These qualities incorporate Courage, Focus, Commitment, Respect, and Openness.

Recommended occasions are utilized in Scrum to make normality and to limit the requirement for gatherings not characterized in Scrum. All occasions are time-boxed. When a Sprint starts, its span is fixed and can't be abbreviated or extended. The rest of the occasions may end at whatever point the motivation behind the occasion is accomplished, guaranteeing a proper measure of time is spent without permitting waste all the while. The Scrum Events are:

Run

Run Planning

Every day Scrum

Run Review

Run Retrospective

Scrum Artifacts

Scrum's relics speak to work or incentive to give straightforwardness and chances to review and adjustment. Ancient rarities characterized by Scrum are explicitly intended to boost straightforwardness of key data with the goal that everyone has a similar comprehension of the relic. The Scrum Artifacts are:

Item Backlog

Dash Backlog

Augmentation

Scrum is a system that assists groups with cooperating. Much like a rugby crew (where it gets its name) preparing for the major event, Scrum urges groups to learn through encounters, self-arrange while taking a shot at an issue, and think about their successes and misfortunes to ceaselessly improve.

While the Scrum I'm discussing is most as often as possible utilized by programming advancement groups, its standards and exercises can be applied to a wide range of collaboration. This is one reason Scrum is so well known. Regularly thought of as a coordinated undertaking the executives system, Scrum portrays a lot of gatherings, apparatuses, and jobs that work in show to assist groups with organizing and deal with their work.

"The Scrum Master is a worker head for the Scrum Team," as indicated by the official Scrum Guide. "[...] liable for advancing and supporting Scrum as characterized in the Scrum Guide. Scrum Masters do this by helping everybody comprehend Scrum hypothesis, practices, rules, and qualities."

Individuals regularly think Scrum and light-footed are something very similar on the grounds that Scrum is revolved around consistent improvement, which is a center guideline of spry. Be that as it may, Scrum is a structure for completing work, where nimble is a mentality. You can't generally "go lithe", as it takes devotion from the entire group to change the manner in which they consider conveying an incentive to your clients. In any case, you can utilize a structure like Scrum to assist you with beginning reasoning that route and to work on building spry standards into your regular correspondence and work.

The scrum structure is heuristic; it depends on ceaseless learning and acclimation to fluctuating elements. It recognizes that the group doesn't know it all toward the beginning of a task and will advance through understanding. Scrum is organized to help groups normally adjust to changing conditions and client necessities, with reprioritization incorporated with the procedure and short discharge cycles so your group can continually learn and improve.

The scrum structure

While Scrum is organized, it isn't totally inflexible. Its execution can be custommade to the requirements of any association. There are numerous hypotheses about how precisely scrum groups must function so as to be fruitful. Notwithstanding, after over a time of helping coordinated groups complete work at Atlassian, we've discovered that unmistakable correspondence, straightforwardness, and a commitment for persistent improvement ought to consistently stay at the focal point of whatever system you pick. What's more, the rest is up to you.

We should begin with recognizing the three antiquities in scrum. Antiquities are something that we make, similar to an instrument to tackle an issue. In Scrum, these three antiquities are an item build-up, a dash overabundance, and an addition with your meaning of "done". They are the three constants in a scrum group that we proceed to return to and put resources into additional time.

Item Backlog is the ace rundown of work that requirements to complete kept up by the item proprietor or item supervisor. This is a powerful rundown of highlights, necessities, upgrades, and fixes that goes about as the contribution for the dash build-up. It is, basically, the group's schedule. The item build-up is continually returned to, re-organized and kept up by the Product Owner in light of the fact that, as we find out more or as the market changes, things may never again be significant or issues may get explained in different manners.

Dash Backlog is the rundown of things, client stories, or bug fixes, chose by the improvement group for execution in the present run cycle. Prior to each run, in the run arranging meeting (which we'll talk about later in the article) the group picks which things it will chip away at for the dash from the item excess. A run build-up might be adaptable and can develop during a run. Be that as it may, the basic dash objective — what the group needs to accomplish from the present run — can't be undermined.

Addition (or Sprint Goal) is the usable final result from a run. At Atlassian, we for the most part exhibit the "increase" during the finish of-dash demo, where the group shows what was finished in the run. You may not hear "increase" out on the planet, as it's regularly alluded to as the group's meaning of "Done", an achievement, the run objective, or even a full form or a delivered epic. It just relies upon how your groups characterizes "Done" and how you characterize your run objectives. For instance, a few groups decide to discharge something to their clients toward the finish of each dash. So their meaning of 'done' would be 'delivered'. In any case, this may not be practical of different kinds of groups. Let's assume you chip away at a server-based item that can just ship to your clients each quarter. You may at present decide to work in 2-week dashes, yet your meaning of 'done' might be completing piece of a bigger form that you intend to transport together. Obviously, the more it takes to discharge programming, the higher the hazard that product will come up short.

As should be obvious, there are loads of varieties, even inside curios, that your group can decide to characterize. That is the reason it's imperative to be stay open to advancing how you keep up even your ancient rarities. Maybe your meaning of 'done' gives fix weight in your group, and you have to return and pick another definition.

You ought to be similarly as light-footed with your structure as you are with your item. Set aside the fundamental effort to monitor how things are going, make alterations if necessary, and don't compel something only for consistency.

Scrum services or occasions

A portion of the more notable segments of the Scrum system are the arrangement of successive occasions, services or gatherings that scrum groups perform all the time. The functions are the place we see the most varieties for groups. For instance, a few groups find doing these services awkward and dreary, while others use them as a fundamental check in. Our recommendation is to begin utilizing the entirety of the services for two dashes and perceive how it feels. You would then be able to play out a speedy retro and see where you may need to modify.

The following is a rundown of all the key functions a scrum group may participate in:

Compose the build-up: Sometimes known as overabundance prepping, this occasion is the obligation of the item proprietor. The item proprietor's principle occupations are to drive the item towards its item vision and have a consistent heartbeat available and the client. Hence, he/she keeps up this rundown utilizing input from clients and the improvement group to help organize and keep the rundown perfect and fit to be taken a shot at some random time. You can peruse progressively about keeping up a sound excess here.

Run arranging: The work to be performed (scope) during the present run is arranged during this gathering by the whole advancement group. This gathering is driven by the scrum ace and is the place the group settles on the run objective. Explicit use stories are then added to the run from the item accumulation. These accounts consistently line up with the objective and are additionally settled upon by the scrum group to be attainable to execute during the dash.

Toward the finish of the arranging meeting, each scrum part should be sure about what can be conveyed in the run and how the addition can be conveyed.

Dash: A run is the real timespan when the scrum group cooperates to complete an augmentation. Two weeks is a really run of the mill length for a run, however a few groups see seven days as simpler to scope or a month to be simpler to convey an important addition. Dave West, from Scrum.org prompts that the more mind boggling the work and the more questions, the shorter the run ought to be. Yet, it's truly up to your group, and you shouldn't be reluctant to transform it if it's not working! During this period, the extension can be re-consulted between the item proprietor and the improvement group if essential. This structures the core of the experimental idea of scrum.

Every one of the occasions — from wanting to review — occur during the dash. When a specific time interim for a run is set up, it needs to stay predictable all through the advancement time frame. This enables the group to gain from past encounters and apply that knowledge to future dashes.

Day by day Scrum or Stand Up: This is a day by day super-short gathering that occurs simultaneously (generally mornings) and spot to keep it straightforward. Numerous groups attempt to finish the gathering in a short time, however that is only a rule. This gathering is likewise called a 'day by day stand-up' underlining that it should be a speedy one. The objective of the day by day scrum is for everybody in the group to be in agreement, lined up with the run objective, and to get a plan out for the following 24 hours.

The stand up is an ideal opportunity to voice any worries you have with meeting the run objective or any blockers.

A typical method to direct a stand up is for each colleague to responds to three inquiries with regards to accomplishing the dash objective:

• What did I do yesterday?

• What do I intend to do today?

• Are there any snags?

Be that as it may, we've seen the gathering rapidly divert into individuals perusing from their schedules from yesterday and for the following day. The hypothesis behind the stand up is that it continue diverting jabber to a day by day meeting, so the group can concentrate on the work for the remainder of the day. So on the off chance that it transforms into an every day schedule read-out, don't be hesitant to switch things up and get imaginative.

Run audit: At the finish of the run, the group gets together for a casual session to see a demo of, or examine, the addition. The advancement group grandstands the accumulation things that are currently 'Done' to partners and colleagues for criticism. The item proprietor can choose whether or not to discharge the addition, despite the fact that by and large the augmentation is discharged.

This survey meeting is additionally when the item proprietor modifies the item overabundance dependent on the present dash, which can sustain into the following run arranging session. For a one-month run, consider time-boxing your dash audit to a limit of four hours.

Run review: The review is the place the group meets up to report and talk about what worked and what didn't work in a run, a venture, individuals or connections, instruments, or in any event, for specific functions. The thought is to make a spot where the group can concentrate on what went well and what should be improved for whenever, and less about what turned out badly.

A scrum group needs three explicit jobs: item proprietor, scrum ace, and the improvement group. Furthermore, in light of the fact that scrum groups are cross-practical, the improvement group incorporates analyzers, architects, UX pros, and operations designs notwithstanding engineers.

Item proprietors are the bosses for their item. They are centered around getting business, client, and market prerequisites, at that point organizing the work to be finished by the designing group in like manner. Viable item proprietors:

Manufacture and deal with the item excess.

Intently band together with the business and the group to guarantee everybody comprehends the work things in the item excess.

Give the group clear direction on which highlights to convey straightaway.

Choose when to dispatch the item with an inclination towards increasingly visit conveyance.

The item proprietor isn't generally the item administrator. Item proprietors center around guaranteeing the advancement group conveys the most incentive to the business. Likewise, it's significant that the item proprietor be a person. No improvement group needs blended direction from numerous item proprietors.

The scrum ace

Scrum aces are the victors for scrum inside their groups. They mentor groups, item proprietors, and the business on the scrum procedure, and search for approaches to adjust their act of it.

A viable scrum ace profoundly comprehends the work being finished by the group and can enable the group to streamline their straightforwardness and conveyance stream. As the facilitator-in-boss, he/she plans the required assets (both human and calculated) for dash arranging, stand-up, run survey, and the run review.

The scrum advancement group

Scrum groups complete s*%&. They are the bosses for reasonable improvement rehearses. The best scrum groups are very close, co-found, and typically five to seven individuals. One approach to work out the group size is to utilize the renowned 'two pizza rule' instituted by Jeff Bezos, the CEO of Amazon (the group ought to be little enough to share two pizzas).

Colleagues have varying ranges of abilities, and broadly educate one another so nobody individual turns into a bottleneck in the conveyance of work. Solid scrum groups are self-sorting out and approach their activities with an unmistakable 'we' frame of mind. All individuals from the group help each other to guarantee a fruitful dash fulfillment.

The scrum group drives the arrangement for each run. They estimate how much work they accept they can finish over the cycle utilizing their verifiable speed as a guide. Keeping the cycle length fixed gives the advancement group significant input on their estimation and conveyance process, which thus makes their figures progressively exact after some time.

Scrum is such a prominent coordinated structure, that scrum and light-footed are frequently misconstrued to be something very similar. Be that as it may, there are different structures, as kanban, which is a well known other option. A few organizations even decide to pursue a half and half model of scrum and kanban, which has gained the name of 'Scrumban' or

Kanplan, which is Kanban with an accumulation.

Both scrum and kanban use visual strategies, for example, the scrum board or kanban board to follow the advancement of work. Both stress proficiency and parting complex errands into littler lumps of reasonable work, however their methodologies towards that objective is unique.

Scrum centers around littler, fixed-length emphasess. When the timeframe for a run is concluded, the accounts or item build-up passages that can be executed during this dash cycle are then decided. In kanban, in any case, the quantity of errands or the work in progress (WIP limit) to be executed in the present cycle is fixed from the start. The time taken to execute these highlights is then determined in reverse.

Kanban isn't as organized as scrum. Other than as far as possible, it is genuinely open to translation. Scrum, in any case, has a few straight out ideas upheld as a component of its execution, for example, dash survey, review, day by day scrum, and so forth. It likewise demands cross-usefulness, which is the capacity of a scrum group to not rely upon outer individuals to accomplish their objectives. Assembling a cross-utilitarian group isn't direct. In that sense, kanban is simpler to adjust while scrum can be considered as a crucial move in the point of view and working of an improvement group.

In any case, why scrum?

The scrum system itself is straightforward. The principles, relics, occasions, and jobs are straightforward. Its semi-prescriptive methodology really helps expel the ambiguities in the advancement procedure, while giving adequate space for organizations to acquaint their individual flavor with it.

The association of complex errands into sensible client stories makes it perfect for troublesome tasks. Likewise, the unmistakable division of jobs and arranged occasions guarantee that there is straightforwardness and aggregate possession all through the improvement cycle. Brisk discharges keep the group roused and the clients cheerful as should be obvious progress in a short measure of time.

Be that as it may, Scrum could take some effort to ace, particularly if the improvement group is acclimatized to a run of the mill cascade model. The ideas of littler emphasess, every day scrum gatherings, dash surveys, and recognizing a scrum ace could be a difficult social move for another group.

Be that as it may, the long haul benefits far exceed the underlying expectation to absorb information. Scrum's achievement in creating complex equipment and programming items crosswise over differing enterprises and verticals makes it a convincing structure to embrace for your association.

Scrum is such an unmistakable composed structure, that scrum and swift are habitually confused to be something fundamentally the same as. In any case, there are various structures, as kanban, which is a notable other choice. A couple of associations even choose to seek after a creamer model of scrum and kanban, which has picked up the name of 'Scrumban' or Kanplan, which is Kanban with a collection.

What is Scrum Project Management?

Scrum is a light-footed undertaking the board strategy or structure utilized essentially for programming advancement ventures with the objective of conveying new programming ability each 2 a month. It is one of the methodologies that affected the Agile Manifesto, which verbalizes a lot of qualities and standards to direct choices on the best way to create better programming quicker.

Who Uses Agile Scrum Methodology?

Scrum is broadly utilized by programming advancement groups. Truth be told it's the most well known nimble procedure. As per the twelfth yearly State of Agile report, 70% of programming groups use Scrum or a

Scrum cross breed. In any case, Scrum has spread to different business capacities including IT and showcasing where there are ventures that must push ahead within the sight of unpredictability and vagueness. Administration groups are likewise putting together their dexterous administration rehearses with respect to Scrum, frequently joining it with lean and Kanban rehearses (subgroups of coordinated task the executives).

What is Scrum in Relation to Agile Project Management?

Scrum is a sub-gathering of nimble:

Nimble is a lot of qualities and rules that portray a gathering's everyday collaborations and exercises. Lithe itself isn't prescriptive or explicit.

The Scrum strategy pursues the qualities and standards of deft, however incorporates further definitions and determinations, particularly with respect to certain product improvement rehearses.

Albeit created for light-footed programming advancement, spry Scrum turned into the favored structure for nimble task the board by and large and is some of the time just alluded to as Scrum venture the board or Scrum improvement.

What are the Benefits Received from the Scrum Methodology?

Associations that have embraced lithe Scrum have encountered:

Higher efficiency

Better-quality items

Decreased time to showcase

Improved partner fulfillment

Better group elements

More joyful representatives

What is So Special About Scrum Project Management?

Scrum tends to multifaceted nature in work by making data straightforward, with the goal that individuals can review and adjust dependent on current conditions, as opposed to anticipated conditions. This enables groups to address the regular traps of a cascade improvement process: tumult coming about because of continually evolving necessities; underestimation of time, assets and cost; settles on programming quality; and wrong progress announcing. Straightforwardness of regular terms and measures is required in Scrum improvement to guarantee that what is being conveyed is what was normal. Visit assessment guarantees progress and identifies fluctuations from the get-go with the goal that modifications can be made rapidly. The most widely recognized Scrum occasions for investigation and adjustment are: Sprint Planning, Daily Scrum or "Stand Up", Sprint Review, and Sprint Retrospective (see Scrum Events beneath).

What is Scrum Methodology Compared to Other Agile Approaches?

Most undertakings first change singular groups to deft before they "scale" to the remainder of the association. Scaling dexterous isn't simple, which has as of late incited new systems to rise, for example, the Scaled Agile Framework® and Disciplined Agile Delivery (DAD) This ubiquity has made Scrum a huge bit of numerous spry application lifecycle the executives (light-footed ALM) activities.

What Are the Components of Agile Scrum Development?

The Scrum system is characterized by group jobs, occasions (functions), antiquities, and rules.

The Scrum Team

Scrum groups are normally made out of 7 +/ - 2 individuals and have no group chief to designate undertakings or choose how an issue is tackled. The group as a unit chooses how to address issues and tackle issues. Every individual from the Scrum group is a vital piece of the arrangement and is required to convey an item from beginning to fruition. There are three key jobs in a Scrum group:

The Product Owner

The Product Owner is the venture's key partner - normally an inside or outer client, or a representative for the client. There is just a single Product Owner who passes on the general strategic vision of the item which the group is building. The Product Owner is eventually responsible for dealing with the item accumulation and tolerating finished augmentations of work.

The ScrumMaster

The ScrumMaster is the hireling chief to the Product Owner, Development Team and Organization. With no hierarchial authority over the group but instead to a greater degree a facilitator, the ScrumMaster guarantees that the group holds fast to Scrum hypothesis, practices, and rules. The ScrumMaster secures the group by doing anything conceivable to enable the group to perform at the most elevated level. This may incorporate evacuating obstructions, encouraging gatherings, and helping the Product Owner man of the hour the excess.

The Development Team

The Development Team is a self-arranging, cross-practical gathering equipped with the entirety of the aptitudes to convey shippable augmentations toward the finish of each dash. Scrum widens the meaning of the expression "designer" past software engineers to incorporate any individual who partakes in the formation of the conveyed augmentation. There are no titles in the Development Team and nobody, including the ScrumMaster, advises the Development Team how to transform item excess things into possibly shippable additions

Scrum Events (Ceremonies)

The Sprint

A run is a period boxed period during which explicit work is finished and prepared for audit. Runs are typically 2 a month long yet can be as short as multi week.

Dash Planning Sprint

Arranging group gatherings are time-boxed occasions that figure out which item overabundance things will be conveyed and how the work will be accomplished.

The Daily Stand-up

The Daily Stand-up is a short correspondence meeting (close to 15 minutes) in which each colleague rapidly and straightforwardly covers progress since the last stand-up, arranged work before the following gathering, and any obstructions that might be hindering their advancement.

The Sprint Review

The Sprint Review is the "sharing time" or exhibition occasion for the group to show the work finished during the dash. The Product Owner checks the neutralize pre-characterized acknowledgment criteria and either acknowledges or dismisses the work. The partners or customers offer input to guarantee that the conveyed addition met the business need.

The Retrospective

The Retrospective, or Retro, is the last group meeting in the Sprint to figure out what went well, what turned out poorly, and how the group can improve in the following Sprint. Gone to by the group and the ScrumMaster, the Retrospective is a significant open door for the group to concentrate on its general execution and distinguish techniques for persistent enhancement for its procedures.

Scrum Artifacts

Item Backlog

The item excess is the absolute most significant record that blueprints each necessity for a framework, venture or item. The item accumulation can be thought of as a plan for the day comprising of work things, every one of which creates a deliverable with business esteem. Accumulation things are requested as far as business esteem by the Product Owner.

Run Backlog

A run build-up is the particular rundown of things taken from the item excess which are to be finished in a run.

Addition

An Increment is the whole of all item build-up things that have been finished since the last programming discharge. While it is up to the Product Owner to choose when an addition is discharged, it is the group's duty to ensure everything that is incorporated into an augmentation is fit to be discharged. This is likewise alluded to as the Potentially Shippable Increment (PSI).

Scrum Rules

The guidelines of dexterous Scrum ought to be totally up to the group and represented by what works best for their procedures. The best dexterous mentors will advise groups to begin with the fundamental scrum occasions recorded above and afterward assess and adjust dependent in your group's interesting needs so there is nonstop improvement in the manner groups cooperate.

Understanding the Agile Framework

WHAT IS AGILE?

Dexterous programming improvement alludes to a gathering of programming advancement approachs dependent on iterative advancement, where prerequisites and arrangements develop through joint effort between self-sorting out cross-useful groups. Coordinated strategies or Agile forms for the most part advance a taught undertaking the executives procedure that empowers visit review and adjustment, an administration reasoning that energizes cooperation, self-association and responsibility, a lot of designing best rehearses planned to take into account fast conveyance of excellent programming, and a business approach that adjusts improvement to client needs and friends objectives. Lithe advancement alludes to any improvement procedure that is lined up with the ideas of the Agile Manifesto. The Manifesto was created by a gathering fourteen driving figures in the product business, and mirrors their experience of what approaches do and don't work for programming improvement.

The agile methodology presented numerous advantages which were unrealistic in the conventional cascade improvement approach, for example, conveying high-esteem includes inside short conveyance cycles. Light-footed improves the degrees of consumer loyalty and client maintenance. The testing is coordinated with improvement in nimble which conveys top notch programming. The numerous advantages offered by dexterous made it progressively mainstream and prompted an across the board selection.

Agile programming advancement procedure is increasingly versatile to changes as there is no inside and out arranging toward the start of a venture rather there are changing prerequisites over the span of the undertaking. A consistent criticism from the end clients is energized. In light-footed, there is a gradual and iterative improvement approach. The work is organized based on business or client esteem. There are cross-utilitarian groups that work on the emphasess of the item over some stretch of time. Every cycle is centered around creating a working item.

Lithe is a system and there are different ways to deal with actualize light-footed.

Scrum

It's one of the most mainstream approaches to execute lithe. In this iterative methodology, there are runs that last one to about fourteen days and enable the group to convey programming on normal premise. Scrum utilizes a product model that pursues a lot of jobs, obligations, and gatherings.

Kanban

In this methodology, a visual structure is utilized to actualize deft. This methodology advances little yet nonstop changes to the present framework. The standards of Kanban incorporate picturing work process, constraining work in progress, overseeing and upgrading the work process and consistent improvement.

Outrageous Programming (XP)

Outrageous Programming centers around improving the quality and responsiveness to developing client necessities. Its standards incorporate criticism, straightforwardness, and grasping change.

Highlight Driven Development (FDD)

FDD includes 5 essential exercises: build up the general model, form a component list, plan by highlight, structure by highlight, and work by highlight. FDD mixes the businesses best practices into a solitary methodology.

Versatile System Development (ASD)

ASD approach centers around the possibility that the venture ought to consistently be in a condition of nonstop adjustment. There is a cycle of 3 rehashing arrangement: hypothesize, team up and learn in ASD.

Dynamic Systems Development Method (DSDM)

DSDM is a way to deal with address its regular disappointments ventures, such as missing cutoff times, going over spending plan and no client inclusion. This methodology centers around the business, being stringent about the practicality, joint effort, never settling on quality, form and grow iteratively, convey consistently and show control.

Lean Software Development (LSD)

Lean Software Development approach (LSD) has 7 standards. These standards incorporate an end of any waste, concentrating on learning, accept choices as late as could be allowed, conveying as quickly as time permits, enabling the group, building respectability and seeing the entire picture.

Completely clear

Completely clear approach is utilized with groups of six to eight engineers. This methodology centers around the individuals engaged with the venture, not procedures or relics. In this procedure, conveyance of usable code to the client is visit. The productivity improvement and correspondence is accomplished by being co-found.

What is Scrum?

Scrum is the most prevalent way to deal with execute light-footed. It oversees programming advancement with an iterative methodology. There are fixed-length emphasess known as a run that permits shipping programming regularly. A run keeps going one to about fourteen days and toward the finish of each run, the partners and colleagues lead a gathering to design the subsequent stages.

The jobs, duties, and gatherings are fixed in a Scrum. In each run, there is run arranging, every day stand-up, run demo and run review. There are task sheets and burndown outlines to catch up on the advancement of the run just as to get steady input.

What is Scrum

Scrum is a deft improvement technique utilized in the advancement of Software dependent on an iterative and gradual procedures. Scrum is versatile, quick, adaptable and powerful spry structure that is intended to convey an incentive to the client all through the improvement of the venture. The essential goal of Scrum is to fulfill the client's need through a situation of straightforwardness in correspondence, aggregate duty and ceaseless advancement. The improvement begins from a general thought of what should be fabricated, explaining a rundown of qualities requested by need (item build-up) that the proprietor of the item needs to get.

The historical backdrop of Scrum can be followed back to 1986 in the Harvard Business Review (HBR) article titled, "The

New Product Development Game" by Hirotaka Takeuchi and Ikujiro Nonaka. This article portrays how organizations, for example, Honda, Canon, and Fuji-Xerox produce new items overall utilizing an adaptable and group based way to deal with item advancement. This methodology accentuates the significance of engaging self-sorted out groups.

In 1993, Jeff Sutherland and his group at Easel Corporation made the Scrum procedure to be utilized in programming advancement forms by consolidating the ideas of the 1986 article with the ideas of item arranged improvement, exact procedure control, iterative advancement and gradual, programming procedures and profitability improvement, just as the advancement of mind boggling and dynamic frameworks.

"Doing half of something is, basically, sitting idle." – Jeff SutherlandCLICK TO TWEET

Scrum Methodology and Process

Scrum is decisively a development of Agile Management. Scrum strategy depends on a lot of characterized practices and jobs that must be included during the product advancement process. It is an adaptable approach that rewards the use of the 12 spry standards in a setting concurred by all the colleagues of the item.

Scrum is executed in brief hinders that are short and intermittent, called Sprints, which generally run from 2 to about a month, which is the term for criticism and reflection. Each Sprint is an element in itself, that is, it gives a total result, a variety of the last item that must have the option to be conveyed to the customer with the least conceivable exertion when mentioned.

The procedure has as a beginning stage, a rundown of targets/necessities that make up the task plan. It is the customer of the task that organizes these goals considering an equalization of the worth and the expense thereof that is the manner by which the emphasess and resulting conveyances are resolved.

From one perspective the market requests quality, quick conveyance at lower costs, for which an organization must be extremely deft and adaptable in the advancement of items, to accomplish short improvement cycles that can fulfill the need of clients without undermining the nature of the outcome. It is an extremely simple technique to actualize and well known for the snappy outcomes it gets.

Scrum technique is utilized for the most part for programming advancement, however different divisions are additionally exploiting its advantages by actualizing this procedure in their hierarchical models, for example, deals, showcasing, and HR groups and so on.

Scrum Development

Various Roles in Scrum

In Scrum, the group centers around building quality programming. The proprietor of a Scrum venture centers around characterizing what are the attributes that the item should need to manufacture (what to fabricate, what not and in what request) and to defeat any deterrent that could ruin the undertaking of the improvement group.

The Scrum group comprises of the accompanying jobs:

Scrum ace: The individual who drives the group managing them to agree to the standards and procedures of the system. Scrum ace deals with the decrease of obstructions of the undertaking and works with the Product Owner to expand the ROI. The Scrum Master is responsible for staying up with the latest, giving instructing, tutoring and preparing to the groups on the off chance that it needs it.

Item proprietor (PO): Is the delegate of the partners and clients who utilize the product. They center around the business part and is liable for the ROI of the task. They Translate the vision of the venture to the group, approve the advantages in stories to be fused into the Product Backlog and organize them all the time.

Group: A gathering of experts with the fundamental specialized information who build up the task together doing the narratives they focus on toward the beginning of each dash.

The Agile Manifesto

The 12 standards of the Agile Manifesto:

Consumer loyalty is of most elevated need which is accomplished through the consistent conveyance of significant programming.

Suit changing necessities even in later periods of advancement.

Convey working programming as often as possible in a shorter timescale.

Business group and engineers must team up every day all through the undertaking.

Higher independence is given to the colleagues with more prominent help and trust.

Eye to eye association is basic for passing on data inside an improvement group.

The advancement of the task is estimated by working programming.

Advance supportable improvement by keeping up a steady pace inconclusively.

Specialized greatness and great configuration ought to be the principle center.

Effortlessness is fundamental for progress.

Self-sorting out groups are required for the best structures and plans.

The groups ought to think about how to turn out to be increasingly viable consistently and embrace the progressions to build adequacy.

"Our most elevated need is to fulfill the client through right on time and consistent conveyance of significant programming". The more drawn out clients need to trust that worth will be conveyed, the more waste will be brought about as far as lost time and lost chance. The business condition will proceed to change, and troublesome contenders may hold onto the activity. On the off chance that a framework is permitted to wander from a developing and emanant set of prerequisites, the almost certain it is to be seen as inadequate when it is at long last discharged. Lean practice depends on conveying the correct worth, to the ideal place, at the ideal time, and at the correct degree of value to fulfill client needs. Prerequisites are a moving objective, and the main thing that really enables us to recalibrate our comprehension is the genuine arrival of significant worth. That is the snapshot of observational truth...and the prior and all the more frequently we convey, the more genuine to client needs we can be.

"Welcome evolving prerequisites, even late being developed. Light-footed forms outfit change for the client's upper hand". The solidifying of prerequisites doesn't solidify economic situations or the earth in which the client works. Additionally, change will happen paying little heed to whether it is caught by examiners. The business condition will proceed to advance, and similarly as doubtlessly, any framework prerequisites will keep on transforming. The alleged fixing of degree just implies that clients need to hold up before an answer in the end unites with their real needs. At that point the condition of the market will have proceeded onward even more, thus the sent framework will be for all time outdated and inadequate. The work done will take care of an inappropriate issue at an inappropriate time, and the client's upper hand stands to be lost. Consequently it is indispensably critical to abstain from solidifying extension, and to oversee necessities change when that change occurs.

"Convey working programming every now and again, from two or three weeks to two or three months, with an inclination to the shorter timescale". The more we delay in discharging programming to clients, the more prominent the act of pure trust we are compelled to take in accepting that the framework will meet their prerequisites. Then again, the more frequently we convey, the less clients need to hold up before working programming gets accessible, and the more outlandish we are to keep putting resources into a framework that is getting progressively unfit for reason. A decent lean methodology is thusly to compel the time we spend before conveying something of significant worth, anyway hardly gradual it might be. This gives us more and better chances to cure any deformities or other non-conformances that develop. In the event that we intentionally take on less work before discharging an augmentation, and rather try to discharge all the more regularly, at that point there will be a diminished possibility for work-in-progress to devalue.

"Specialists and designers must cooperate day by day all through the task". At whatever point an email or comparative notice is sent between agents and designers, there is a postponement in the other party accepting a reaction. The time spent hanging tight for an answer makes the estimation of the discussion deteriorate. Any non-conformance with prerequisites is more averse to be imparted and settled successfully and in time. Additionally, every specially appointed gathering that is set up requests that the participants make plans to be there, which is anything but a beneficial utilization of exertion. For the most slender conceivable work process, it tends to be fitting to have business and specialized individuals cooperate each day as per normal procedure, so that they are quickly accessible to one another, and the estimation of their talks is boosted.

"Assemble extends around inspired people. Give them the earth and bolster they need, and trust them to take care of business". Gifted individuals should go to where the work is, at the time and spot it needs doing. On the off chance that work is passed between them rather, as indicated by their control, proficiency will be lost since that individual may not be prepared to deal with it around then. The manner in which lean activities are organized should mirror a shared feeling of demonstrable skill, where groups review and adjust their way to a concurred result. On the off chance that work apparently is developing in one zone, at that point the group will concentrate on finishing it so as to smooth lean stream. Self-association of this nature can request social change, and consequently it is imperative to help the group in these endeavors.

"The most proficient and compelling technique for passing on data to and inside an improvement group is eye to eye discussion". Having business and designers cooperate can be a significant initial phase in diminishing the time they spend hanging tight for one another's information and input. It likewise decreases the need to set up and go to gatherings. The potential lean efficiencies can be expanded in the event that they all team up eye to eye. Non-verbal signs at that point become accessible to colleagues, and it is simpler for them to convey, create, and seek after a common spotlight on the job needing to be done.

"Working programming is the essential proportion of progress". The customary stage-gated model of programming improvement checks progress by methods for promissory notes. These are regularly the investigation, structure, testing, and the board records which report on whether conveyance is on plan and inside spending plan. Such yields don't in themselves offer some incentive to partners. Best case scenario, they can only guarantee that worth will be conveyed at some future point. The least fatty approach to prove progress is through experimentation, by discharging and utilizing working highlights both early and regularly. Any non-conformances with partner desires would then be able to be uncovered and managed quickly, and the danger of exertion being squandered on ineffective exercises is limited.

"Dexterous forms advance supportable improvement. The supporters, engineers, and clients ought to have the option to keep up a steady pace uncertainly". Whenever sat around idly and exertion is permitted to collect, it gets more enthusiastically to keep up an anticipated pace of significant worth conveyance. Building an inappropriate thing at an inappropriate time saps a group's vitality and speaks to a lost open door for them to do truly helpful work. Over-burdening the group trying to repay isn't practical after some time. Quality will break down, further waste will be brought about, consistency will be lost, and in the end the wheels of the activity may fall off. The need to keep up a reasonable pace in lean practice can barely be overemphasized.

"Persistent regard for specialized greatness and great configuration improves nimbleness". Unaddressed deserts are a typical wellspring of specialized obligation. By giving close consideration to specialized greatness and great plan, consistently, the odds of that obligation developing will be limited. Diminishing the weight of medicinal work improves the capacity of lean professionals to react to change, so ideal worth is conveyed. On the off chance that a group cautiously confines the work it has in progress at any one time, individuals can concentrate better on finishing it to the essential standard.

"Straightforwardness - the craft of expanding the measure of work not done - is basic". Conveying new highlights more rapidly than clients can promptly assimilate is advancement exertion gone to squander. The worth brought by that new capacity can't then be acknowledged, and the venture made in its generation will devalue quickly. The chance to contribute rare assets all the more profitably is likewise lost. Besides, pointless multifaceted nature is acquainted with the framework, and there is currently more to turn out badly. An increasingly cunning practice is to concentrate on the things clients need now, and will be in a situation to utilize. The law of miserliness can be relied upon to hold in a lean method for working. There is a basic to streamline, and to discover "methods for doing less so you can accomplish more".

"The best structures, necessities, and plans rise up out of self-sorting out groups". The worth clients get is just tantamount to the worth stream that produces it. As every augmentation is taken a shot at by a group, its potential worth is expanded. Worth including exercises -, for example, investigation and plan, for instance - are best when lean groups self-sort out around the work and colleagues team up with one another. They can apply shared understanding and joint concentration to the current test, which is addressing client needs in a convenient manner. Every determination a self-sorting out group needs to create, before worth can be discharged, is bound to upgrade the worth clients do in certainty get.

"At normal interims, the group thinks about how to turn out to be increasingly successful, at that point tunes and modifies its conduct in like manner". On the off chance that a work process is to turn out to be really lean, and stay lean, it must be consistently investigated and adjusted. Everything about a work process ought to be available to challenge by the group which possesses it. There is no augmentation they convey, nor any coincidental action they perform, nor any procedure they pursue, which is invulnerable from their thought regarding its observational result.

The three Scrum concept explained

DEFINITION

Scrum

Scrum is a structure for venture the board that underlines collaboration, responsibility and iterative advancement toward a well-characterized objective. The system starts with a basic reason: Start with what can be seen or known. From that point forward, track the advancement and change as fundamental. The three mainstays of Scrum are straightforwardness, review and adjustment. The structure, which is regularly part of Agile programming improvement, is named for a rugby development. Everybody assumes a job. With regards to item improvement, Scrum jobs incorporate item proprietor, Scrum ace and Scrum advancement group.

Item proprietor: This colleague fills in as the contact between the improvement group and its clients. The item proprietor is liable for guaranteeing desires for the finished item have been conveyed and settled upon.

Scrum ace: This colleague fills in as a facilitator. The Scrum ace is answerable for guaranteeing that Scrum best practices are done and the task can push ahead.

Scrum advancement group: This is a gathering that cooperates for making and testing steady arrivals of the last item.

The Scrum procedure urges experts to work with what they have and constantly assess what is working and what isn't working. Correspondence, which is a significant piece of the procedure, is helped out through gatherings, called Events. Scrum Events include:

Every day Scrum . The Daily Scrum is a short stand-up meeting that occurs at a similar spot and time every day. At each gathering, the group surveys work that was finished the earlier day and plans what work will be done in the following 24 hours. This is the ideal opportunity for colleagues to make some noise about any issues that may avert venture finishing.

Run Planning Meeting. A Sprint alludes to the time period wherein work must be finished, and it's frequently 30 days. Everybody takes part in defining the objectives, and toward the end, at any rate one addition - a usable bit of programming - ought to be delivered.

Dash Review. This is an ideal opportunity to flaunt the addition.

Run Retrospective. A Sprint Retrospective is a gathering that is held after a Sprint closes. During this gathering, everybody thinks about the Sprint procedure. A group building activity may likewise be advertised. A significant objective of a Sprint Retrospective is ceaseless improvement.

The Scrum structure shows how the components of Scrum rotate around the Scrum teamSCRUM.ORG

The Scrum structure shows how the components of Scrum spin around the Scrum group.

Scrum antiques

An antique is something of verifiable intrigue that has the right to be taken a gander at once more. In Scrum item advancement, antiquities are utilized to perceive what's been done and what is still in the line. Scrum antiquities, which incorporate item excess, Sprint accumulation, item addition and burn to the ground, are valuable to take a gander at in Sprint Planning Meetings.

Item accumulation. This alludes to what stays on the "to be done" list. During an item accumulation prepping session, the advancement group works with the entrepreneur to organize work that has been multiplied. The item excess might be calibrated during a procedure called overabundance refinement.

Run build-up. This is a rundown of assignments that must be finished before chosen item excess things can be conveyed. These are separated in to time sensitive client stories.

Item increase. This alludes to what's been cultivated during a Sprint - all the item excess things - just as what's been made during every single past Sprint. The item increase reflects how much progress has been made.

Burn to the ground. The torch is a visual portrayal of the measure of work that still should be finished. A torch diagram has a Y pivot (work) and a X hub (time). In a perfect world, the diagram outlines a descending pattern, as the measure of work still left to do after some time torches to zero.

The historical backdrop of Scrum

The reason for the Scrum structure in programming improvement was first presented in 1986 by Hirotaka Takeuchi and Ikujiro Nonaka in an article distributed by The Harvard Business Review. In the article, which was entitled "The New Product Development Game," the writers utilized allegories to depict two distinct ways to deal with overseeing item advancement. A few groups resembled sprinters in a hand off race, passing the rod along, working in a straight line. Different groups were rugby players, playing a solitary game and passing things to and fro, as essential.

Takeuchi and Nonaka finished up the hand off race approach, as exemplified by the NASA Phased Program Planning framework, was obsolete. They accepted the rugby style would give organizations the devices important to contend in a worldwide business world.

Jeff Sutherland, John Scumniotales and Jeff McKenna are said to have attempted Scrum programming advancement at Easel Corp. in 1993. In 1995, Ken Schwaber and Sutherland, working with others - including McKenna and Scumniotales - exhibited a persuasive white paper at OOPSLA, entitled

"SCRUM Development Process." The outcome was an ocean change that made engineers question the viability of the exemplary Waterfall programming improvement model. As indicated by Scrum.org, over 70% of every single Agile group today use Scrum or a Scrum crossover.

Scrum esteems

The mainstays of scrum

The three mainstays of Scrum - straightforwardness, investigation and adjustment - are upheld by five qualities: duty, fortitude, center, receptiveness and regard.

Responsibility: The group is self-coordinated, and all individuals are devoted to finishing work that has been settled upon.

Fearlessness: The group works as a solitary element and succeeds or flops together.

Center: as far as possible interruptions and focuses on what work should be done today.

Receptiveness: The group is offered time to assemble and share what has been effective and what should be improved.

Regard: The group is made out of individuals who have various qualities, and every individual's qualities are regarded. There is no blame dispensing while examining how to fix what isn't functioning.

Comprehend where Scrum fits in the range of programming advancement

Discover the advancement philosophy that works best for you

Figure out how an ALM center can help with Scrum forms

Guidance for producing prerequisites in Agile Scrum

Study venture arranging and the executives

Related Terms

lithe promoting

Lithe promoting is an iterative way to deal with showcasing procedures that models techniques utilized in spry programming improvement.

meaning of done

A meaning of done is an agenda of criteria that an item, item augmentation or task must fulfill to be considered .

dash (programming advancement)

A dash is a set timeframe during which explicit work must be finished and prepared for audit.

Benefits of Scrum

Following are ten significant benefits that scrum gives to associations, groups, items, and people. To exploit scrum benefits, you have to trust in observation, discover progressively about the scrum structure by utilizing it, and persistently review and adjust your execution of scrum.

Better quality

Tasks exist to achieve a dream or objective. Scrum gives the system to nonstop criticism and presentation to ensure that quality is as high as could reasonably be expected. Scrum guarantees quality by the accompanying practices:

Characterizing and explaining on necessities without a moment to spare so information on item includes is as significant as could be expected under the circumstances

Joining day by day testing and item proprietor criticism into the advancement procedure, permitting the improvement group to address issues while they're new

Normal and ceaseless improvement of scrum group yield (item or administration) through run audits with partners

Directing dash reviews, permitting the scrum group to consistently improve such group explicit factors as procedures, devices, connections, and workplaces

Finishing work utilizing the meaning of done that tends to improvement, testing, joining, and documentation

Diminished time to advertise

Scrum has been demonstrated to convey an incentive to the end client 30 to 40 percent quicker than conventional techniques. This abatement in time is because of the accompanying elements:

Prior inception of improvement because of the reality the forthright documentation periods of cascade ventures (which regularly take months) are inevitable by having a committed item proprietor installed inside the scrum group to dynamically expand necessities "without a moment to spare" and give continuous explanation.

Most noteworthy need necessities are isolated from lower-need things. Steadily conveying an incentive to the end client implies that the -highest-esteem and -hazard prerequisites can be conveyed before the lower-worth and hazard necessities. No compelling reason to hold up until the whole venture is finished before discharging anything into the market.

Usefulness is swarmed to finish each dash. Toward the finish of each run, scrum groups produce working item and administration augments that are shippable.

Expanded degree of profitability

The reduction so as to showcase is one key explanation that scrum ventures understand a better yield on speculation (ROI). Since income and other focused on benefits start coming in sooner, prior aggregation implies higher absolute return after some time. This is an essential precept of net present worth (NPV) computations. Notwithstanding time-to-showcase benefits, ROI with scrum likewise increments by

Ordinary input through dash surveys legitimately from partners, including clients, empowers course rectifications early, which is less expensive and tedious than later simultaneously.

Less expensive imperfections because of mechanization and direct front testing implies less squandered work and quicker arrangements.

Diminishing expenses of disappointment. In the event that a scrum venture will come up short, it flops prior and quicker than cascade ventures.

Higher consumer loyalty

Scrum groups are focused on delivering items and administrations that fulfill clients. Scrum empowers more joyful task supports through the accompanying:

Teaming up with clients as accomplices and keeping clients included and connected all through ventures.

Having an item proprietor who is a specialist on item prerequisites and client needs.

Keeping the item build-up refreshed and organized to react rapidly to change.

Exhibiting working usefulness to inner partners and clients in each dash survey.

Conveying item to end clients quicker and more regularly with each discharge instead of at the same time at the end.

Steadily subsidizing tasks as opposed to requiring huge in advance responsibilities.

Higher camaraderie

Working with cheerful individuals who make the most of their occupations can be fulfilling and fulfilling. Self-administration puts choices that would regularly be made by a chief or the association into scrum colleagues' hands. Scrum improves the spirit of colleagues in these manners:

Being a piece of a self-overseeing and self-arranging group enables individuals to be imaginative, creative, and recognized for their aptitude.

Advancement groups may sort out their group structure around individuals with explicit work styles and characters.

Scrum groups can settle on choices customized to give balance between colleagues' expert and individual lives.

Having a friend association with a business agent (item proprietor) on a similar group adjusts specialized and business needs and separates authoritative hindrances.

Having a scrum ace, who serves the scrum group, evacuates hindrances and shields the improvement group from outside obstructions.

Concentrating on manageable work practices and rhythm guarantees that individuals don't wear out from pressure or exhaust.

Working cross-practically permits improvement colleagues to adapt new aptitudes and to develop by instructing others.

Empowering a hireling head approach helps scrum groups in self-administration and effectively staying away from direction and-control strategies.

Giving a domain of help and trust expands individuals' general inspiration and assurance.

Having eye to eye discussions lessens the dissatisfaction of miscommunication.

At last, scrum groups can concede to rules about how they work to take care of business.

Expanded cooperation and possession

At the point when scrum groups assume liability for activities and items, they can deliver extraordinary outcomes. Scrum groups work together and take responsibility for and venture execution through the accompanying practices:

Having the improvement group, the item proprietor, and the scrum ace work firmly together consistently

Directing run arranging gatherings, permitting the improvement group to sort out its work around educated business needs

Having day by day scrum gatherings where advancement colleagues compose around work finished, future work, and barricades

Leading run surveys, where the item proprietor plots his prioritization choices and the improvement group can exhibit and talk about the item legitimately with partners

Leading dash reviews, permitting scrum colleagues to survey past work and prescribe better rehearses with each run

Working in a colocated domain, taking into account moment correspondence and coordinated effort among advancement colleagues, the item proprietor, and the scrum ace

Settling on choices by agreement

Progressively important measurements

The measurements that scrum groups use to evaluate time and cost, measure venture execution, and settle on venture choices are frequently more important and more precise than measurements on conventional undertakings. On scrum ventures, measurements are progressively pertinent on the grounds that

The individuals who will take the necessary steps, and nobody else, give exertion evaluations to extend prerequisites.

Courses of events and spending plans depend on every advancement group's genuine exhibition and abilities.

Utilizing relative appraisals, as opposed to hours or days, tailors evaluated exertion to an individual improvement group's information and abilities.

In under one moment daily, designers can refresh the torch outline, giving day by day perceivability of how the advancement group is advancing toward a dash objective.

Toward the finish of each dash, an item proprietor can look at the undertaking's real cost (AC) in addition to the open door cost of future activities (OC) against the worth that the present task is returning (V) to realize when to end a venture and start another one. You don't have to hold up until the finish of a venture to recognize what its worth is.

Improved progress perceivability and presentation

On scrum extends, each individual from the undertaking group (which incorporates the scrum group and partners) has the chance to know how the venture is going at some random time. Straightforwardness and perceivability make scrum an introduction model to enable the venture to group precisely recognize issues and all the more precisely foresee how things will go as the task advances. Scrum activities can give an elevated level of progress perceivability by

Putting a high incentive on open, genuine correspondence among the scrum group, partners, clients, and any other individual inside an association who needs to think about an undertaking.

Day by day scrums that give day by day knowledge into the improvement group's prompt advancement and barriers.

Day by day scrums around task sheets empower engineers to self-arrange and distinguish the most elevated need errands for the afternoon.

Utilizing the data from every day scrum gatherings, run torch diagrams, and errand sheets permits the task group to follow progress for singular runs.

Run reviews permit scrum colleagues to recognize what's functioning admirably and what's not to make activity arrangements for development.

Showing achievements in run audits. Anybody inside an association may go to a dash audit, even individuals from other scrum groups.

Expanded venture control

Scrum groups have various chances to control venture execution and make revisions as required as a result of the accompanying practices:

Modifying needs all through the task at each dash interim instead of at significant achievements enables the association to have fixed-time and fixed-value ventures while pleasing change.

Grasping change permits the venture group to respond to outside factors like market request.

Every day scrum coordination permits the scrum group to rapidly address issues as they emerge, and swarm together to complete necessities to.

Every day updates to run overabundances imply that dash torch graphs precisely reflect run progress, allowing the scrum group the chance to make changes the minute it sees issues.

Up close and personal discussions evacuate barriers to correspondence and issue goals.

Run audits let venture partners see working items and give item proprietors the criticism they have to ensure the safety.

Scrum rules

Scrum is an iterative Agile programming advancement strategy for overseeing undertakings and item or application improvement. These days, Scrum has been utilized by everybody from advertising organizations to development teams. Whenever you're beginning another undertaking, be it programming or an email crusade, Scrum can assist you with sorting out your group and accomplish more work in less time.

Here is a brisk manual for the most basic standards for Scrum gatherings and Scrum sheets that you ought to never break.

Scrum Meetings

#1. All colleagues are required to go to Scrum gatherings

In the event that a colleague can't go to face to face, s/he should report their work status by telephone (or by some other methods) or request that an associate make a report for them. Everybody ought to be liable for what has been finished.

#2. Continuously appear on schedule

The Scrum ace will begin the gathering at the selected time, in any case whether you are available or not. So be expeditious on the off chance that you would prefer not to miss significant updates.

#3. At the point when you're having a gathering, just a single individual talk one after another

Just the person who gives an account of their status! Worth your time and don't squander it on silly discussions.

#4. Notwithstanding the quantity of colleagues, week by week Scrum gatherings ought to be no longer than 15-30 minutes.

#5. Each colleague ought to react to three questions

What have you done since the last week by week scrum meeting?

What will you do from this point until the following week after week meeting?

What snags hinder you from playing out your work?

#6. In the event that a report by any colleague brings up extra issues or causes discourses, every invested individual ought to get together after the week after week scrum meeting.

Scrum Board

#1. Clingy notes

Each office should have clingy notes of a specific shading and record the proprietor and due date on them. It's likewise a decent practice to list the undertaking name, customer names, and so forth.

#2. Checking area

This is the piece of the load up where you characterize every important asset (time, materials, and so on.) that are important to finish the task.

#3. Accumulation area

The accumulation incorporates every one of your ventures and undertakings that are on your daily agenda in 2 a month. These things ought to be refreshed each week so the whole group comprehends what's on the plan.

#4. Stopping area

This is the place you keep ventures (thoughts for improving undertakings) that are occurring in 3-6 months.

#5. Dash area

This area addresses the inquiry "what am I doing this week?" If there is a thing that ought to be conveyed during this week, it has a place with the dash.

#6. QA area

This is the place your things/ventures/errands are anticipating for endorsement or input from a customer.

#7. Finished area

This is the place your task/thing gets when it's endorsed by the customer.

The Scrum core roles

A significant component of SCRUM is minimal number of jobs. These Roles have direct impact on the acknowledgment of a venture. The SCRUM center jobs are accepted to be responsible for the creation of expectations which meet the acknowledgment criteria in each dash which thusly guarantees accomplishment of the whole venture.

Coming up next are the three head jobs in Scrum:

The Product Owner-is the voice of the business,

The Development Team-that changes over thoughts into usefulness

The Scrum Master - who empowers the group and procedure

The Product Owner

The item proprietor is respected to be the person who has far-sightedness of the venture and is responsible for gathering the necessities and requirements to comprehend the estimation of the task.

The item proprietor is likewise liable for managing and posting the item build-up. He is likewise engaged with the arranging of the discharge.

An item Owner is regularly the venture chief or can likewise be a business examiner who has specialized abilities. An effective item proprietor is required to have qualities, for example, abundant specialized information, needs to have area expertize and ought to be effectively open to the advancement group.

The Scrum Master

The Scrum Master has his/her attention on the advancement of the procedure and furthermore is known to manage the scrum group.

The Scrum Master is answerable for arranging the dashes and organizing the run build-up. He/she is likewise associated with overseeing improvement process. The Scrum Master likewise helps in recognizing and taking out the deterrents that is as of now blocking the exhibition of the group

The Scrum Master is answerable for setting up the torch outline and aides in immaculate correspondence among everyone in the undertaking. The scrum ace empowers the gathering to pursue the work process and guarantees that the errands in the dashes are finished on schedule. A Scrum Master can either be the group chief or go about as the task director. A scrum ace is undeniably considered to have a decent equalization of abilities, for example, specialized skill, issue solver, cooperative person and an issue solver.

The Scrum Team

A Scrum group doesn't mean the commonplace advancement group. A scrum group has its own extraordinary abilities.

Expressed beneath are hardly any highlights of a Scrum group

Cross-utilitarian groups: the group has individuals from different teaches so as to help accomplish the affirmed capacities. Programming engineers, software engineers, designers, investigators, framework administrators, analyzers and so on could be the individuals from the groups.

Self-arranging groups: the groups accept an approach assignment to be finished by whom and how to finish the undertakings.

Business portrayal: The business delegate is as the voice of the client, and furthermore the voice of progress.

Build-up driven: work is done according to the overabundance.

The duties of the improvement group:

Accomplish dash objectives

To set self-up made objectives

To sort out their time

Scrum processes

Scrum forms address the particular exercises and stream of a Scrum venture. Altogether there are 19 procedures in SBOK® Guide which are gathered into following five stages:

Start - This stage incorporates the procedures identified with inception of an undertaking: Create Project Vision, Identify Scrum Master and Stakeholder(s), Form Scrum Team, Develop Epic(s), Create Prioritized Product Backlog, and Conduct Release Planning. More

Plan and Estimate - This stage comprises of procedures identified with arranging and evaluating assignments, which incorporate Create User Stories, Approve, Estimate, and

Commit User Stories, Create Tasks, Estimate Tasks, and Create Sprint Backlog. More

Actualize - This stage is identified with the execution of the errands and exercises to make an undertaking's item. These exercises incorporate making the different expectations, leading Daily Standup Meetings, and prepping (i.e., auditing, adjusting, and consistently refreshing) the Product Backlog at standard interims. More

Audit and Retrospect - This stage is worried about exploring the expectations and the work that has been done and deciding approaches to improve the practices and strategies used to do extend work. More

Discharge - This stage stresses on conveying the Accepted Deliverables to the client and recognizing, reporting, and disguising the exercises picked up during the task.

The Scrum model recommends that undertakings progress by means of a progression of runs. With regards to a coordinated system, dashes are timeboxed to close to a month long, most regularly two weeks.

Scrum technique advocates for an arranging meeting toward the beginning of the run, where colleagues make sense of what number of things they can focus on, and afterward make a run build-up – a rundown of the assignments to perform during the run.

During a dexterous Scrum run, the Scrum group takes a little arrangement of highlights from thought to coded and tried usefulness. Toward the end, these highlights are done, which means coded, tried and coordinated into the advancing item or framework.

On every day of the run, all colleagues ought to go to a day by day Scrum meeting, including the ScrumMaster and the item proprietor. This gathering is timeboxed to close to 15 minutes. During that time, colleagues share what they chipped away at the earlier day, will take a shot at that day, and recognize any obstructions to advance.

The Scrum model considers every day to be as an approach to synchronize crafted by colleagues as they examine crafted by the run.

Toward the finish of a run, the group leads a run audit during which the group exhibits the new usefulness to the PO or whatever other partner who wishes to give criticism that could impact the following dash.

This input circle inside Scrum programming improvement may bring about changes to the newly conveyed usefulness, yet it might similarly as likely outcome in reconsidering or adding things to the item accumulation.

Another movement in Scrum venture the board is the dash review toward the finish of each run. The entire group takes an interest in this gathering, including the

ScrumMaster and PO. The gathering is a chance to think about the dash that has finished, and recognize chances to improve.

Scrum Process: The Main Artifacts

The essential ancient rarity in Scrum advancement is, obviously, the item itself. The Scrum model anticipates that the group should carry the item or framework to a possibly shippable state toward the finish of every Scrum dash.

The item overabundance is another relic of Scrum. This is the finished rundown of the usefulness that remaining parts to be added to the item. The item proprietor organizes the accumulation so the group consistently takes a shot at the most important highlights first.

The most prevalent and fruitful approach to make an item excess utilizing Scrum procedure is to populate it with client stories, which are short depictions of usefulness portrayed from the point of view of a client or client.

In Scrum venture the executives, on the primary day of a run and during the arranging meeting, colleagues make the dash overabundance. The run build-up can be thought of as the group's plan for the day for the run, while an item build-up is a rundown of highlights to be fabricated (written as client stories).

The run overabundance is the rundown of errands the group needs to perform so as to convey the usefulness it resolved to convey during the dash.

Extra relics coming about because of the Scrum dexterous strategy is the run burndown outline and discharge burndown diagram. Burndown graphs show the measure of work remaining either in a dash or a discharge, and are a compelling instrument in Scrum programming improvement to decide if a run or discharge is on calendar to have all arranged work wrapped up by the ideal date.

The Agile Scrum Project: Main Roles

Regardless of whether you are new to Scrum, you may have known about a job called the ScrumMaster. The ScrumMaster is the group's mentor, and enables Scrum experts to accomplish their most elevated level of execution.

In the Scrum procedure, a ScrumMaster contrasts from a customary undertaking administrator from numerous points of view, including that this job doesn't give everyday course to the group and doesn't relegate errands to people.

A decent ScrumMaster covers the group from outside interruptions, permitting colleagues to concentrate derangedly during the dash on the objective they have chosen.

While the ScrumMaster centers around helping the group be as well as can be expected be, the item proprietor attempts to guide the group to the correct objective. The item proprietor does this by making a convincing vision of the item, and afterward passing on that vision to the group through the item overabundance.

The item proprietor is answerable for organizing the excess during Scrum improvement, to guarantee it's satisfactory as more is found out about the framework being constructed, its clients, the group, etc.

The third and last job in Scrum venture the board is simply the Scrum group. In spite of the fact that people may get the group together with different occupation titles, in Scrum, those titles are immaterial. Scrum philosophy expresses that every individual contributes in the manner they can to finish crafted by each dash.

This doesn't imply that an analyzer will be required to re-draftsman the framework; people will burn through most (and now and then the entirety) of their time working in whatever control they worked before receiving the deft Scrum model. In any case, with Scrum, people are relied upon to work past their favored controls at whatever point doing so would be to benefit the group.

One approach to think about the interlocking idea of these three jobs in this spry system is as a racecar.

The Scrum group is simply the vehicle, prepared to speed along toward whatever path it is pointed. The item proprietor is the driver, ensuring that the vehicle is continually going the correct way. What's more, the ScrumMaster is the main technician, keeping the vehicle all around tuned and performing at its best.

Before the genuine improvement in Scrum there is additionally obviously the task arranging and the plan of the harsh design.

In the task arranging, determinations for the venture are characterized: for instance, which representatives take part, what advancement devices are utilized and what shows ought to be clung to. In this specific circumstance, the principal form of the Product Backlog (assortment of the necessities) will likewise be made. This can occur before the genuine Scrum process or be on the whole turned out by the Scrum Team inside the structure of a first Sprint.

The Actual Process

Graph 10 shows the Scrum procedure, the characterized ancient rarities and furthermore the booked gatherings:

The Scrum Process

Graph 10: The Scrum Process

Gatherings and Artifacts

The Scrum procedure is rehearsed in different gatherings and accordingly gives a few ancient rarities which are depicted underneath.

The Product Backlog

The Product Owner makes a rundown of prerequisites dependent on the portrayal of advantages — the Product Backlog. The request for the sections simultaneously sets their need. The entirety of the Stakeholders add to its substance. This not just occurs toward the start of an improvement and at specific occasions, however as an on-going procedure. When change demands or new prerequisites rise, they are embedded into the Product Backlog. This principal receptiveness to acknowledge steady changes and view them not as deterrents however as circumstances, prompts high adaptability in the advancement. The prioritization is frequently founded on the altruism estimation of the business or on a hazard associated with the necessity. This takes into consideration snappy response to changing conditions without risking the venture.

A Product Backlog can, for instance, have the accompanying structure:

Model Scrum Product Backlog

Table 1: Example Product Backlog

The Sprint Planning Meeting and the Sprint Backlog

The Sprint Planning Meeting happens toward the start of a Sprint and all undertaking individuals take part. This is the place the Team and the Product Owner settle on the substance of the following Sprint.

The Product Owner characterizes the most elevated need sections ("Items") of the Product Backlog and clarifies their practical use. The Team assesses the exertion of the "Things".

The Team chooses the "Things" for a Sprint from the Product Backlog as per the prioritization and afterward places them into the Sprint Backlog.

When the Team and Product Owner concur with the execution of the Sprint Backlog in the following Sprint, the Sprint Goal is characterized.

From that point forward, the Team includes the Sprint Backlog "Things" to a usage plan. These are for the most part explicit advancement exercises.

The Sprint at that point begins. For dependability, the necessities of the Sprint Backlog ought not change during a Sprint.

The Impediment List

When the main Sprint has begun, each Team Member can include the supposed hindrances (Blockers) to a rundown. Each Team Member reports their Blocker for the execution of an assignment when it emerges and puts it in the rundown of Blockers. It is the assignment of the Scrum Master to dispose of these Blockers. A Blocker might be a system condition, yet could likewise be the sit tight for an incomplete assignment. The Blocker is passed on to the next Team Members in the Daily Scrum Meeting and recorded in the Impediment List.

Case of an Impediment List:

Case of a Scrum Impediment List

Table 2: Example of an Impediment List

Table 2 speaks to a case of an Impediment List. Further sections can obviously be included. Where appropriate, a status for every line could be beneficial if the rundown ought not just incorporate remarkable Blockers.

The Daily Scrum Meeting

When a Sprint has begun, the Team meets at the Daily Scrum Meeting. The Daily Scrum Meeting is a casual gathering enduring greatest 15 minutes. In this gathering, each colleague needs to respond to the accompanying three inquiries:

What did I do yesterday that helped the Development Team meet the Sprint Goal?

What will I do today to enable the Development To group meet the Sprint Goal?

Do I see any hindrance that anticipates me or the Development Team from meeting the Sprint Goal?

This gathering isn't a broad exchange, however the groups short every day arranging meeting to facilitate the vital undertakings to arrive at the run objective.

It is the Scrum Master's assignment to guarantee this occurs.

The Scrum Master's primary assignment is to determine developing Blockers. His undertaking isn't to control the Team. The Team is self-sorting out.

The accompanying rules apply to the "Day by day Scrum":

The gathering consistently begins on schedule.

The gathering ought to consistently happen in a similar area and simultaneously.

The gathering will be held transparently, everybody can take an interest, yet the real jobs have select talking rights.

The gathering is constantly restricted to a limit of 15 minutes, paying little heed to the size of the Team.

The members should remain during the gathering. This should help keep the gathering brief.

The Sprint Review Meeting/Retrospective

Toward the finish of each Sprint there is a "Survey Meeting", in which the Team shows the outcomes to the Product Owner and different Stakeholders. Everybody can take an interest in this gathering and give criticism on the outcomes and their improvement. An audit of the Sprint (the review) likewise happens toward the finish of a Sprint. The entire Scrum Team is welcome to this. What ought to be improved later on is talked about at this gathering.

The Goal of the Sprint

A chief estimation of Scrum is the capacity to incorporate new prerequisites into the framework after every emphasis and Sprint. With each progression the client gets an executable framework which, over the span of time, turns out to be progressively similar to the final result. Not at all like other iterative advancement models, Scrum centers around executable frameworks, yet additionally on really usable frameworks. In this way, the improvement of a total framework ought not be isolated into singular modules that can't reasonably be utilized without the total framework. This dodges the client not getting an item which can really be utilized by the clients until the finish of the advancement procedure and afterward having change demands emerge. The guideline here is that the client ought not get what he has indicated however what he very. The prioritization of the necessities as indicated by the altruism estimation of the business additionally guarantees that the client can utilize his most significant capacities at a beginning period.

What is Scrum Project Management?

Scrum is a coordinated undertaking the board philosophy or structure utilized fundamentally for programming improvement ventures with the objective of conveying new programming ability each 2 a month. It is one of the methodologies that impacted the Agile Manifesto, which expresses a lot of qualities and standards to manage choices on the most proficient method to create better programming quicker.

Who Uses Agile Scrum Methodology?

Scrum is generally utilized by programming advancement groups. Indeed, it's the most prevalent dexterous system. As indicated by the twelfth yearly State of Agile report, 70% of programming groups use Scrum or a

Scrum cross breed. Notwithstanding, Scrum has spread to different business capacities including IT and advertising where there are ventures that must push ahead within the sight of multifaceted nature and uncertainty. Authority groups are likewise putting together their lithe administration rehearses with respect to Scrum, regularly consolidating it with lean and Kanban rehearses (subgroups of deft task the board).

What is Scrum in Relation to Agile Project Management?

Scrum is a sub-gathering of lithe:

Lithe is a lot of qualities and rules that depict a gathering's everyday collaborations and exercises. Light-footed itself isn't prescriptive or explicit.

The Scrum philosophy pursues the qualities and standards of spry, yet incorporates further definitions and determinations, particularly with respect to certain product improvement rehearses.

Albeit produced for lithe programming improvement, coordinated Scrum turned into the favored system for nimble venture the executives as a rule and is now and again basically alluded to as Scrum venture the board or Scrum advancement.

What are the Benefits Received from the Scrum Methodology?

Associations that have received dexterous Scrum have encountered:

Higher profitability

Better-quality items

Diminished time to advertise

Improved partner fulfillment

Better group elements

More joyful workers

What is So Special About Scrum Project Management?

Scrum tends to intricacy in work by making data straightforward, with the goal that individuals can review and adjust dependent on current conditions, as opposed to anticipated conditions. This enables groups to address the normal traps of a cascade improvement process: disarray coming about because of continually evolving necessities; underestimation of time, assets and cost; settles on programming quality; and wrong progress revealing. Straightforwardness of regular terms and guidelines is required in Scrum advancement to guarantee that what is being conveyed is what was normal. Visit review guarantees progress and identifies differences at an opportune time so alterations can be made rapidly. The most well-known Scrum occasions for assessment and adjustment are: Sprint Planning, Daily Scrum or "Stand Up", Sprint Review, and Sprint Retrospective (see Scrum Events beneath).

What is Scrum Methodology Compared to Other Agile Approaches?

Most undertakings first progress singular groups to deft before they "scale" to the remainder of the association. Scaling lithe isn't simple, which has as of late provoked new structures to develop, for example, the Scaled Agile Framework® and Disciplined Agile Delivery (DAD) This fame has made Scrum a critical bit of numerous light-footed application lifecycle the board (dexterous ALM) activities.

What Are the Components of Agile Scrum Development?

The Scrum philosophy is characterized by group jobs, occasions (services), relics, and rules.

The Scrum Team

Scrum groups are commonly made out of 7 +/ - 2 individuals and have no group head to designate undertakings or choose how an issue is illuminated. The group as a unit chooses how to address issues and take care of issues. Every individual from the

Scrum group is a basic part of the arrangement and is relied upon to convey an item from origin to consummation. There are three key jobs in a Scrum group:

The Product Owner

The Product Owner is the venture's key partner - normally an inside or outer client, or a representative for the client. There is just a single Product Owner who passes on the general strategic vision of the item which the group is building. The Product Owner is eventually responsible for dealing with the item build-up and tolerating finished additions of work.

The ScrumMaster

The ScrumMaster is the hireling head to the Product Owner, Development Team and Organization. With no hierarchial authority over the group yet rather all the more a facilitator, the ScrumMaster guarantees that the group clings to Scrum hypothesis, practices, and rules. The ScrumMaster secures the group by doing anything conceivable to enable the group to perform at the most significant level. This may incorporate expelling hindrances, encouraging gatherings, and helping the Product Owner lucky man the accumulation.

The Development Team

The Development Team is a self-sorting out, cross-practical gathering equipped with the entirety of the aptitudes to convey shippable additions toward the fulfillment of each dash. Scrum expands the meaning of the expression "engineer" past software engineers to incorporate any individual who partakes in the making of the conveyed addition. There are no titles in the Development Team and nobody, including the ScrumMaster, advises the Development Team how to transform item excess things into possibly shippable augmentations

Scrum Events (Ceremonies)

The Sprint

A dash is a period boxed period during which explicit work is finished and prepared for audit. Dashes are normally 2 a month long yet can be as short as multi week.

Run Planning Sprint

Arranging group gatherings are time-boxed occasions that figure out which item excess things will be conveyed and how the work will be accomplished.

The Daily Stand-up

The Daily Stand-up is a short correspondence meeting (close to 15 minutes) in which each colleague rapidly and straightforwardly covers progress since the last stand-up, arranged work before the following gathering, and any obstacles that might be obstructing their advancement.

The Sprint Review

The Sprint Review is the "sharing time" or show occasion for the group to exhibit the work finished during the run. The Product Owner checks the neutralize pre-characterized acknowledgment criteria and either acknowledges or dismisses the work. The partners or customers offer input to guarantee that the conveyed addition met the business need.

The Retrospective

The Retrospective, or Retro, is the last group meeting in the Sprint to figure out what went well, what turned out poorly, and how the group can improve in the following Sprint. Gone to by the group and the ScrumMaster, the Retrospective is a significant open door for the group to concentrate on its general execution and recognize systems for consistent enhancement for its procedures.

Scrum artifacts

Scrum Artifacts give key data that the Scrum Team and the partners should know about for understanding the item being worked on, the exercises being arranged, and the exercises done in the venture. The accompanying relics are characterized in Scrum Process Framework.

Item Vision

Dash Goal

Item Backlog

Dash Backlog

Meaning of Done

Torch Chart

Augmentation

Torch Chart

Other required ancient rarities...

Note That:

These are the most well-known antiques in a scrum extend and venture curios are not constrained by these.

Best Scrum Software

Best Scrum Software Every Project Needs

An incredible scrum programming that supports scrum venture the executives. It highlights scrum devices like client story map, item build-up the board, dash overabundance the executives, task the board, day by day scrum meeting, run arranging apparatus, run audit device, run review instrument, burndown, hindrance, partner and group the board.

Find out More

Item Vision

The Product Vision is a curio to characterize the long haul objective of the task/item. It sets the general course and aides the Scrum Team. Everybody ought to have the option to retain the Product Vision; thusly it must be short and exact.

Run Goal

The Sprint Goal centers the Sprint. The target will be met inside the Sprint through the execution of the anticipated Product Backlog things, and it gives direction to the Development Team on why it is building the Product Increment.

According to the Scrum Guide, the obligation regarding making a Sprint Goal is for the Scrum Team. It is anyway in huge piece important to the Product Owner to help this procedure by having clear business objectives for the coming Sprint, which can likewise make requesting the Product Backlog significantly simpler by giving Focus.

Item Backlog

An item build-up is a rundown of the considerable number of things that are required in the item and it is a dynamic and best comprehended prerequisite for any progressions to be made to the item. Item accumulation possessed by the Product Owner (PO) which comprises of a rundown all highlights, capacities, prerequisites, upgrades, and fixes that establish the progressions to be made to the item later on discharges.

Item accumulation

Item accumulation

Commonly, the prerequisites of an item continue evolving, for example change in business necessities, economic situations, or innovation. Consequently, item excess is reliably refreshed to reflect what the item should be generally valuable to the objective clients.

Dash Backlog

The Sprint Backlog is the arrangement of Product Backlog things chose for the Sprint in addition to an arrangement for conveying the item Increment and understanding the Sprint Goal. The Sprint Backlog is a gauge by the Development Team about what usefulness will be in the following Increment and the work expected to convey that usefulness. The Sprint Backlog characterizes the work the Development Team will perform to transform Product Backlog things into a "Done" Increment. The Sprint Backlog makes obvious the entirety of the work that the Development Team distinguishes as important to meet the Sprint Goal.

Dash build-up

Dash build-up

Meaning of Done

Each Product Backlog thing has acknowledgment criteria that characterize quantifiably what must be met when the thing is proclaimed to be finished. Numerous criteria apply to all or numerous Product Backlog things. Rather than more than once characterizing these criteria with everything, it has demonstrated to be helpful to gather these criteria in a single spot: the Definition of Done. Consequently, the Definition of Done is a common comprehension of the Scrum Team on the importance of work to be finished. It regularly contains quality criteria, limitations and generally speaking non-useful necessities. Here are a few models:

Meaning of Done (DOD)

Meaning of Done (DOD)

Addition

The Increment is the whole of all the Product Backlog things finished during a Sprint and every past Sprint.

Toward the finish of a Sprint, the new Increment must be "Done," which implies:

It must meet the Scrum Team's Definition of "Done."

It must be in usable condition paying little mind to whether the Product Owner chooses to really discharge it.

The Burndown Chart

Burndown diagrams are charts that give a review of progress after some time while finishing a task. As assignments are finished, the diagram "burns to the ground" to zero. It is utilized as an instrument to direct the advancement group to an effective fulfillment of a Sprint on time with a working last item. On the off chance that a group chooses they have moved a greater number of goals than feasible for finish from the Product Backlog to the Sprint Backlog, the Burndown Chart can help them is discovering which undertakings they are not practically ready to finish with the goal that these assignment can be moved back to the Product Backlog.

In a co-found Scrum group, curios assume an imperative job for the group to think about themselves how they are getting along with the run objective. Relics characterized by Scrum are explicitly intended to augment straightforwardness of key data with the goal that everyone has a similar comprehension of the relic.

Per the most recent Scrum direct, Scrum system characterizes 3 fundamental antiquities.

Curio #1: Product Backlog

The Product excess is a lot of all gauge necessities organized all together which is made accessible by the Product Owner to the Scrum Team. The item excess rises and advances after some time and the Product Owner is answerable for its substance and legitimacy.

The Product build-up is a living antiquity that might be exposed to change, when there is an adjustment in the outer business condition, economic situations, administrative changes or innovation changes.

Scrum groups chip away at the Product build-up and make a conceivably shippable item increase which is demoed to the client. The input from the client is annexed to the Product overabundance.

Item Backlog refinement, additionally prevalently known as Backlog prepping, is a casual Scrum group function that happens each dash, where everybody in the group, including Scrum Master and Product Owner party to guarantee that work things in the excess are significant and helpful, and everything adjusts to the general item guide. It is for sure all the more a working session than a run of the mill shut entryway meeting.

Normal exercises during the accumulation refinement are

Checking on the most elevated need stories on the highest point of the excess

Approach inquiries to item proprietor for more data.

Erasing stories that are never again required

Composing new client stories

Re-organizing and power positioning the tales

Re-characterize the acknowledgment criteria

Making new client stories when vital

Assessing or re-evaluating stories

Re-evaluating the general need of stories

Breaking the sagas further into client stories

Refining stories to prepare for future dashes

Comprehend the changing greater image of the item engineering as the accumulation rises.

Ancient rarity #2: Sprint Backlog

The Sprint Backlog is a subset of the Product Backlog that the group destroys into the run to take a shot at. It is basically the rundown of "To Do's" an improvement group may be working during the present run.

The work things in the Sprint Backlog are separated further into errands by the group. All things on the Sprint Backlog ought to be created, tried, reported and coordinated to satisfy the responsibility.

The Sprint overabundance arrangement is generally guided by the Sprint Goal. It is a gauge by the improvement group on what usefulness the group should work and convey.

The Product Owner encourages the group to come up the dash objective during the run arranging meeting.

The Sprint overabundance can be changed by the Scrum group as it advances. The improvement group may talk about the work in progress during the Daily Scrum and adjust the Sprint Backlog all through the Sprint, as the Sprint Backlog develops during the Sprint.

As new work is required, the Development Team adds it to the Sprint Backlog. As work is performed or finished, the assessed remaining work is refreshed. At the point when components of the arrangement are regarded superfluous, they are expelled.

Just the Development Team can change its Sprint Backlog during a Sprint. The Sprint Backlog is an exceptionally unmistakable, constant image of the work that the Development Team intends to achieve during the Sprint, and it has a place exclusively with the Development Team.

Antiquity #3: Product Increment

The most significant Scrum antiquity is the Product Increment. Each Sprint the advancement group creates conceivably shippable item increase. This item increase must adjust to the advancement group's "Meaning of Done" and this addition must be adequate by the Product Owner.

This item increase must be the whole of all the Product Backlog things finished during the present dash and the estimation of the additions delivered during the entirety of the past runs. The Product increase must be in a usable condition paying little mind to when the Product Owner chooses to really discharge it.

The Product augmentation is a bit of working programming that makes straightforwardness to every one of the partners. The group may likewise make other discretionary extra antiques like copy down diagrams and undertaking sheets

Meaning of Done

At the point when the Product Increment is conveyed, it needs to meet "Meaning of Done" which is a common understanding report of the advancement group in regards to of what "done" signifies. This definition is diverse for each Scrum Team, and as the group develops, the Definition of Done will grow and turn out to be increasingly stringent

Scrum's curios speak to work or incentive in different manners that are valuable in giving straightforwardness and chances to investigation and adjustment. Antiques characterized by Scrum are explicitly intended to amplify straightforwardness of key data expected to guarantee Scrum Teams are effective in conveying a "Done" Increment.[23]

Item Backlog:

The Product Backlog is an arranged rundown of everything that may be required in the item and is the single wellspring of prerequisites for any progressions to be made to the item. The Product Backlog is rarely finished, it just spreads out the known and best got prerequisites. Item Backlog is dynamic, it reliably changes to recognize what the item should be helpful.

The Product Backlog records all highlights, capacities, necessities, improvements, and fixes that establish the progressions to be made to the item later on discharges. As item is utilized and gains esteem, input is given and the Backlog increases. Necessities change constantly. Changes in business necessities, economic situations, or innovation may cause changes in the Product Backlog.

Checking Progress Toward a Goal:

Whenever, the absolute work staying to arrive at the objective can be added. Different projection rehearses have been utilized to gauge progress, however whats will happen is obscure. Just what has happened can be use for forward-looking basic leadership.

Run Backlog:

The Sprint Backlog is the arrangement of Product Backlog things chose for the Sprint in addition to an arrangement for conveying the item Increment and understanding the Sprint Goal. The Sprint Backlog is an estimate by the Development Team about what usefulness will be in the following Increment and the work expected to convey that usefulness. The Sprint Backlog characterizes the work the Development Team will perform to transform Product Backlog things into a "Done" Increment. The Sprint Backlog makes unmistakable the entirety of the work that the Development Team distinguishes as important to meet the Sprint Goal. [23]

Observing Sprint Progress:

Improvement group tracks absolute work staying at any rate for each Daily Scrum. Improvement group tracks these aggregates day by day and activities probability of accomplishing the Sprint Goals.

Addition:

The Increment is the whole of all the Product Backlog things finished during a Sprint and every past Sprint. Toward the finish of a Sprint, the new Increment must be "Done," which implies it must be in usable condition and meet the Scrum Team's Definition of "Done." It must be in usable condition paying little mind to whether the Product Owner chooses to really discharge it.

Scrum flow

Scrum Flow

A Scrum venture begins with a dream of the framework to be created. The vision may be dubious from the outset, maybe expressed in showcase terms as opposed to framework terms, however it will become more clear as the task pushes ahead. The Product Owner is dependable to those subsidizing the task for conveying the vision in a way that boosts their ROI. The Product Owner details an arrangement for doing so that incorporates a Product Backlog. The Product Backlog is a rundown of utilitarian and nonfunctional necessities that, when transformed into usefulness, will convey this vision. The Product Backlog is organized with the goal that the things well on the way to create esteem are top need and is isolated into proposed discharges. The organized Product Backlog is a beginning stage, and the substance, needs, and gathering of the Product Backlog into discharges as a rule changes the minute the task begins—as ought not out of the ordinary. Changes in the Product Backlog reflect changing business prerequisites and how rapidly or gradually the Team can change Product Backlog into usefulness.

All work is done in Sprints. Each Sprint is a cycle of 30 back to back schedule days. Each Sprint is started with a Sprint arranging meeting, where the Product Owner and Team get together to work together about what will be accomplished for the following Sprint. Choosing from most elevated need Product Backlog, the Product Owner tells the Team what is wanted, and the

Team tells the Product Owner the amount of what is wanted it trusts it can transform into usefulness throughout the following Sprint. Run arranging gatherings can't last longer than eight hours—that is, they are time-boxed to maintain a strategic distance from an excess of hand-wringing about what is conceivable. The objective is to get the opportunity to work, not to consider working.

The Sprint arranging meeting has two sections. The initial four hours are gone through with the Product Owner displaying the most noteworthy need Product Backlog to the Team. The Team interrogates that person concerning the substance, reason, which means, and expectations of the Product Backlog. At the point when the Team knows enough, yet before the initial four hours slips by, the Team chooses as a lot of Product Backlog as it trusts it can transform into a finished augmentation of conceivably shippable item usefulness before the finish of the Sprint. The Team focuses on the Product Owner that it will put forth a valiant effort. During the second four hours of the Sprint arranging meeting, the Team designs out the Sprint. Since the Team is answerable for dealing with its very own work, it needs a provisional arrangement to begin the Sprint. The errands that make this arrangement are put in a Sprint Backlog; the undertakings in the Sprint Backlog rise as the Sprint develops. Toward the beginning of the second four-hour time of the Sprint arranging meeting, the Sprint has begun, and the clock is ticking toward the 30-day Sprint time-box.

Consistently, the group gets together for a 15-minute gathering called a Daily Scrum. At the Daily Scrum, each Team part responds to three inquiries: What have you done on this undertaking since the last Daily Scrum meeting? What do you plan on doing on this task among now and the following Daily Scrum meeting? What obstacles hold up traffic of you meeting your responsibilities to this Sprint and this task? The motivation behind the gathering is to synchronize crafted by all Team individuals day by day and to plan any gatherings that the Team needs to advance its encouraging.

Toward the finish of the Sprint, a Sprint audit meeting is held. This is a four-hour, time-boxed gathering at which the Team presents what was created during the

Sprint to the Product Owner and whatever other partners who need to visit. This casual gathering at which the usefulness is exhibited is proposed to unite individuals and help them cooperatively figured out what the Team ought to do straightaway. After the Sprint audit and preceding the following Sprint arranging meeting, the ScrumMaster holds a Sprint review meeting with the Team. At this three-hour, time-boxed gathering, the ScrumMaster urges the Team to reexamine, inside the Scrum procedure system and practices, its improvement procedure to make it progressively viable and charming for the following Sprint. Together, the Sprint arranging meeting, the Daily Scrum, the Sprint audit, and the Sprint review establish the experimental assessment and adjustment practices of Scrum.

In our ongoing post, "The Scrum Framework: A Guide," we gave a review of Scrum groups and the duties related with every job. This substance proceeds with first experience with Scrum and how groups can utilize it to accomplish proficient, top notch results that limit hazard and augment item conveyance.

In our past substance, we talked about the item overabundance and noticed that it distinguishes the task's long haul needs and records highlights, capacities, necessities, improves and fixes. After an item build-up is made, excess refinement happens. This is an approach to survey and reexamine things so as to include detail, gauges and request. During this procedure, the item advancement group works out the refinement subtleties. The item proprietor can refresh the overabundance refinement whenever.

During dash arranging, the group decides the run objective. The time spent on arranging is significant: gauges from Scrum designers recommend a limit of eight hours for a one-month run, or two hours per week. The arrangement responds to the accompanying inquiries:

What things can be conveyed inside the dash increase?

By what means will the work finished inside this run accomplish the addition objective?

By what means will the picked work complete?

The improvement group chooses what is to be finished inside a dash and how it should function, just as disclosing it to the item proprietor and Scrum ace. It is then the Scrum ace's obligation to ensure the group is taking on a sensible, feasible measure of work and doesn't overcommit. By and large, Scrum Alliance takes note of that "things on the run accumulation are entrusted out so as to give the group certainty that it can finish the thing."

...

Snap To Tweet

The everyday Scrum is a gathering led by the advancement group so as to improve correspondence, wipe out the requirement for different gatherings, recognize barricades and advance speedy basic leadership. These gatherings commonly keep going for 15 minutes and enable the groups to synchronize on exercises finished since the past day by day Scrum, just as conjecture the work that will be done before the following one. Colleagues ordinarily answer addresses, for example,

What did I do yesterday to enable the group to meet our objective?

What will I do today to enable the group to meet our objective?

Are there any bottlenecks or barricades that avert me (or the group) from meeting the objective?

It is the Scrum ace's obligation to encourage the evacuation of any obstructions that would shield the group from accomplishing the objectives of the run. This may require working with different colleagues and different partners. The advancement group frequently meets following the day by day Scrum so as to unlawful input and cultivate cooperation. This empowers them to adjust or re-plan the rest of the work as required.

Run audit gatherings are casual and held toward the finish of the run. During these gatherings, the group examines the work finished during the dash. In light of occasions that happened during the dash itself (for instance, if changes were made to the item build-up) the dialog movements to what should be possible so as to streamline esteem. Run survey is additionally when the item proprietor and group demonstrate the outcomes to partners. They do this to feature the group's advance just as get criticism on what they've finished up until now.

The dash review meeting happens after the run survey and before the following run arranging meeting. It has three purposes: to assess the past dash with respect to individuals, connections, procedures and instruments; to recognize and arrange the things that went well as potential upgrades; and to make an execution plan for the distinguished enhancements. At the point when changes should be made pushing ahead, they are authorized by the Scrum ace in future runs. After the review, the present run is finished and the group starts the following run, discharge or extend as fitting.

Scaling Scrum

Ken Schwaber is best known as the co-maker of scrum, organizer of The Scrum Alliance, and head of Scrum.org. As leader of Advanced Development Methods (ADM), a consultancy that assists associations with improving programming improvement rehearses, he has been discreetly chipping away at Nexus, a guide for scaling scrum in huge scale coordinated tasks. His idea of Scaled Professional Scrum (SPS) structures the center of Nexus, which he portrays as "the exoskeleton of scaled scrum."

TechBeacon got up to speed with Ken to discuss his new accentuation on helping associations scale spry, Nexus, and what comes straightaway.

TB: What are the key difficulties in scaling scrum?

Schwaber: We thought in 2001 we had squashed that approach with The Agile Manifesto, however after ten years methodologists have seen a chance to profit—a great deal of it—through the silver projectile intrigue of prescriptive methodologists and their intrinsic direction and control approach.

At the official level we have had perhaps a 30 percent achievement rate with understanding what deftness truly is, the thing that it requires, what it conveys, and afterward being happy to do the difficult work to fabricate programming that way. In this, coordinated is the same as lean: basic yet hard.

Numerous late adopters start with CIOs that have been told by their CEO that they will be "dexterous" or "scale scrum." These associations have prevailing by improving huge volumes of work through advancing work and exchange stream, sorting out progressively with direction and control and assigned work, and ingrained consistency through nitty gritty forthright arranging.

Nonetheless, deftness and lithe necessitate that we change the manner in which individuals are engaged, trusted, and self-sorted out. That feels abnormal to CIOs and their directors. Emerging prerequisites and ventures driven by clients likewise doesn't feel good. These are better approaches for seeing work.

At the point when light-footed is spoken to by a methodologist in an order and control, prescriptive strategy that can be purchased and executed, this feels right to these associations. Get it, show it, actualize it—it's finished. But it isn't, on the grounds that the premise of spryness is that product improvement, as mind boggling work, can't be institutionalized into one arrangement. Each association and undertaking is one of a kind and requires new arrangements. So when an association that is accustomed to appointing and a methodologist says "give me this cash and you'll be deft," it feels better, it feels right, it fits in.

TB: What results have you seen from this methodology?

Schwaber: We had huge achievement in before years in places like Adobe, Intuit, Cisco, Google, Salesforce.com, and littler organizations that were putting intensely in new items, new thoughts, change, and being better. The possibility of strengthening, change, and lean items were extraordinary. The triumphs made the buzz and force of the lithe development. This caused the business press and meetings to praise the spry development, to distinguish it as the way to programming venture achievement. In any case, despite the fact that these associations see others that have improved, they are agreeable, don't have any basic issues, and are composed and acculturated to prescient, exchange based, progressively oversaw associations. The advantages of nimble might be attractive, however there is nothing squeezing that legitimizes the required work and culture change.

These later associations utilize the conventional methodology. Focus on purchasing an answer that doesn't require culture or designing change, just a difference in structure and classification. Rather than placing in the difficult work of making sense of how spry would function and concocting a consistent improvement intend to arrive, associations are sold coordinated as an implementable format, one size fit all. Rather than the expense being the perspiration value paid by the early associations, these later associations attempt to purchase in.

So, on the off chance that I need consistency and prescriptive and I need coordinated, that is a contention. Scrum is exceptionally simple, but on the other hand it's extremely hard. The hardness is placing individuals in struggle with old propensities to get new outcomes. On the off chance that the issue the association faces aren't so convincing or so horrendous that individuals realize they need to transform, they go with what feels good.

TB: What have you been taking a shot at of late?

Schwaber: We ceaselessly deal with improving our courseware, our preparation, helping individuals to survey their very own abilities. The presentation of things like the Scaled Agile Framework, taught lithe conveyance, and endeavor shared administrations began to reintroduce methodological, prescriptive, one-size-fits-all recollecting into programming advancement, simultaneously guaranteeing that it was nimble. Be that as it may, these methodologies self-destruct at the product advancement level. They ordinarily simply state, "use scrum," however scrum is a one-group, one-dash thing. Likewise, these philosophies don't reveal to you how to run enormous, multi-group scrum ventures or projects.

In a fruitful scrum usage, when associations need to execute huge activities or discharges for up to 3,000 individuals, they devise their very own strategies for working out conditions, cause visit coordination to uncover rotting conditions, and embrace consistent incorporation and assemble. A few undertakings or discharges are normally required to devise satisfactory strategies and tooling, and the association recognizes and works out the issues as ability totals.

These venture strategies share a great deal practically speaking with the old reasonable brought together procedure and counseling—business methodology, stage technique, framework system and transforming those into plans, portfolios, and an item overabundance. That is all great top-down work that is the premise of significant level counseling. I don't know how the organizations executed these things, yet the thoughts were truly useful for their level. What I don't find in those is a lot of spotlight on programming improvement, which is my zone of intrigue. What I didn't see them spread is the way to utilize enormous groups on huge tasks.

What I see with these organizations is that when they get the discharge train (or proportional) down to the improvement level, they arrive and kind of scratch their heads.

So we pulled together a program for scaling. We conceived a structure that would assist associations with running scaled undertakings without forcing prescient strategies that are contradictory to that association.

We developed Nexus, a straightforward structure, an exoskeleton over scrum that empowers up to a 100-man exertion, alongside rules and occasions for how to do as such. We incorporate numerous practices that recognize and evacuate conditions and consistently coordinate work to expel specialized obligation and the dangerous adjustment stage.

Key Takeaways

Scaled Agile works, and utilizing a scaling structure assist you with getting a brisk beginning.

All scaling structures share some normal examples: Scrum at group level, numerous groups sharing a build-up, arranging is done cooperatively crosswise over groups, and the general standards of draw and self-association.

In the event that you realize Scrum truly well, LeSS is the "easy decision" structure for scaling, and you may never require whatever else.

SAFe gives a great deal of direction, and spreads a more extensive degree than different structures, including financing and venture design.

Scrum@Scale recommends not very many practices, yet is a decent apparatus for fitting your very own scaled Agile usage.

You can compose numerous Scrum groups from various perspectives. In this article we analyze LeSS, SAFe, and Scrum@Scale dependent on our work with these systems. There are different structures for scaling Agile, for example, DAD (Disciplined Agile Delivery) and Nexus, however they are not shrouded in this article.

Scaling

As indicated by Craig Larman and Bass Vodde (the makers of LeSS) the essential principle of scaling lithe is: don't do it!

On the off chance that you have issues with:

Cross group conditions

Dangers that influence a few groups

Booking of (composed) conveyances

RELATED VENDOR CONTENT

Highlight Flag Best Practices (By O'Reilly) -
Download the eBook

Ballet performer: A Language for Network-
Distributed Applications (By O'Reilly)

Manual Monitoring Bad! Programmed
Monitoring Good!

Overseeing Feature Flags - Download the eBook (By O'Reilly)

Building Smarter Communications Using Artificial Intelligence

RELATED SPONSOR

RingCentral Developers encourages you upset business correspondences with APIs for voice, SMS, Glip, gatherings, and fax. Begin for nothing.

you may require a scaling system. On the off chance that you can manage these issues by re-organizing your groups and item structure, you are in an ideal situation without one. On the off chance that you can't, it would be ideal if you keep perusing.

What LeSS, SAFe and Scrum@Scale share practically speaking

Every one of the three structures start with cross-practical, self-arranging Scrum groups. The groups vertically cut necessities into the littlest potential augmentations that can be conveyed autonomously. Groups are likewise expected to concentrate on specialized greatness, for example, doing persistent incorporation and mechanized relapse testing. Toward the finish of each run the groups ought to have a possibly deployable item. The three systems likewise urge you to utilize Lean standards to upgrade your stream.

LeSS (Large Scale Scrum)

LeSS is a scaling structure that originates from Craig Larman and Bas Vodde, and depends on their work in the budgetary and media transmission ventures.

LeSS is characterized by moderation and insignificant process, for example use as meager procedure as conceivable to get various Scrum groups to function admirably. LeSS comprises of a handfull of rules, there are additionally aides and models for how to alter these standards as the association develops.

At its most essential level, LeSS is an explanation of how Scrum is planned to function. For instance, it explains that Scrum groups ought to be extensive cross-utilitarian element groups that are kept up over different activities. The thought is to deal with the unpredictability of enormous scale advancement by improving it however much as could be expected. Along these lines, LeSS prescribes that numerous groups has a similar Product Owner and a mutual Product Backlog. Their runs are synchronized to the Product-level Sprint prompting one incorporated Potentially Shippable Product Increment. Run Planning, Sprint Review and Sprint Retrospective runs simultaneously for all groups.

One Product Owner with one item build-up, and a few groups, each with its own dash excess.

It may appear to be unimaginable for a solitary individual to be a Product Owner for up to eight groups, however the way of thinking of LeSS blocks the Product Owner from taking an interest at a detail level, which prompts groups that assume on the liability to work out their very own answers. This powers the engineers to draw nearer to their clients, giving them a superior comprehension of their clients' unique circumstance, needs and issues. The outcome is a more elevated level of contribution and custom arrangements, created with better quality all the more effectively. Basically, you "get more with LeSS".

Outline of LeSS with synchronized dashes.

Procedure savvy, LeSS is unadulterated Scrum (time-boxed cycles, run arranging, every day stand-up, dash audit, and review), with an adjustment. According to Scrum, Sprint Planning is part into two sections. In any case, LeSS suggests that the initial segment is a joint gathering gone to by agents from the entirety of the groups to concur "What" Product Backlog Items (PBIs) will be worked in the coming Sprint. The second piece of Sprint Planning is then utilized by each group to create the Sprint Backlog and concur "How" the PBI's will be fabricated.

Basic dash end for all groups in LeSS

The finish of the dash likewise should be synchronized. This is cultivated by having one normal Sprint Review for every one of the groups. The Retrospective is isolated into two sections, likewise to the run arranging. To begin with, each group holds their very own individual group Retrospective, at that point agents from each group hold a joint Retrospective together that empowers them to distinguish and address gives that can't be tackled at the individual group level.

LeSS Huge

In the event that there are in excess of eight Scrum groups working off a similar item build-up, it's an ideal opportunity to separate the item overabundance into various necessity zones. We at that point dole out 4-8 groups to every one of these new necessity zone explicit overabundances.

Every region has its own Product Owner, knows as an Area Product Owner, and build-up simply like fundamental LeSS. The Product Owner job is as yet present, and that individual is liable for all the item regions. The procedure (Sprint arranging, day by day stand-up, Sprint audit, and Retrospective) is utilized on both the general level and the territory levels.

Item proprietor with his/her Area Product Owners and their groups

SAFe

SAFe is Dean Leffingwell's structure. Form 1 appeared in 2011. By 2016 the structure was up to Version 4, and we expect that it will keep on advancing. We have put together the content beneath with respect to the SAFe Version 4.

Association

SAFe's focal reason is to partition the work into esteem streams. A worth stream comprises of the means that the organization consistently rehashes to convey an incentive to clients and clients. Somewhere in the range of 5 and 15 groups are regularly associated with a worth stream, and this gathering of groups is known as a discharge train. A discharge train can contain up to 150 individuals. When that edge is surpassed it is prescribed to have a few Agile discharge prepares inside each worth stream.

Sprint cycle

To begin a Scrum venture, the Product Owner makes and organizes a rundown of list of things to get things called the item excess. Through the Sprint Planning Meeting, the Scrum Team chooses what number of things from the build-up can be created in a Sprint. Each day of the Sprint, the group get together and do a stand-up assembled the Daily Scrum Conference. During the Sprint, Scrum Master attempts to expel any hindrances and blockers so the Scrum Team can keep on working. Toward the finish of the Sprint, the Team grandstand the created highlights to the group and different partners, which are possibly possibility for discharge. Toward the finish of the Sprint, there is likewise a Sprint Review at the Retrospective Meeting.

The Sprint contains every one of the components of Scrum. It is a touching procedure with one emphasis promptly following the following immediately. While the primary Scrum group utilized a month long Sprint, most groups currently work in a couple of week cycles.

The run starts with Planning and finishes with Review and Retrospective. Every day of the Sprint is set apart by a concise gathering called the Daily Scrum or essentially, Stand-up, as everybody should remain to keep the gathering short.This ordinary cycle:

Conveys on the Sprint Goal. A conceivably shippable augmentation of programming, a useable emphasis of an equipment item, or any conveyance that straightforwardly creates obvious client esteem.

Gives the Team standard, great input on conveyed esteem. The Team would then be able to examine and adjust both their procedure and their item dependent on genuine and significant client input.

Measures Team yield over a reliable and repeating timeframe. This is known as the Team's speed. The Team can utilize this measurement to evaluate the effect of procedure tests.

Dashes start and end on fixed dates. There are no expansions. No progressions can be made to the Sprint Backlog that would jeopardize the Sprint Goal. No extra work ought to be brought into the Sprint except if the Sprint Goal has been come to or an element develops of such high worth it must be brought into Sprint. In this occasion, the Team ought to execute the Interrupt Pattern. In enormous tasks with different Teams, conditions must be deliberately overseen crosswise over groups. Frequently this implies Sprints should start and end on similar dates and have a similar length.

Agile estimation techniques

Here are 7 deft Agile strategies past Planning Poker.

1. Arranging Poker

All members use numbered playing a game of cards and gauge the things. Casting a ballot is done unknown and discourse is raised when there are huge contrasts. Casting a ballot is rehashed till the entire group arrived at agreement about the exact estimation. Arranging poker functions admirably when you need to appraise a relative modest number of things (max 10) in a little group (5-8 individuals). Tip: attempt to keep the democratic between moderate numbers. Boost the most elevated card to 13 points. More on arranging poker by means of this connection.

2. Shirt Sizes

This is an ideal system for assessing a huge build-up of relative huge things. Particularly when you have a few simultaneous scrum groups taking a shot at a similar item. Things are evaluated into shirt sizes: XS, S, M, L, XL. The choice about the size depends on an open and shared community oriented discourse. This strategy is a casual and brisk approach to get an unpleasant inclination about the complete size of your excess. Progressively about T-shirt size estimation is here.

3. Spot Voting

At the point when you are looked with a relative little arrangement of things and needing a very basic and powerful system to assess you can utilize Dot Voting. This strategy has begun structure basic leadership and you can utilize it for evaluating. Every individual gets few little stickers and can decide to decide in favor of the individual things. The more specks is a marker of a greater size. Functions admirably in both little and huge gathering. You need to restrain the quantity of evaluated things. More on spot casting a ballot here.

4. The Bucket System

A lot quicker than arranging poker is the Bucket System. This framework is a decent elective when evaluating an enormous number of things with a huge gathering of members. Make a few cans in the grouping of arranging poker. The gathering gauges the things by setting them in these "basins". Containers are normally various sheets of darker paper where you can put the clingy note with the thing. In any case, you can likewise utilize real crates to confine dialog about effectively prepared things. More on the pail technique here.

5. Enormous/Uncertain/Small

A very quick strategy for harsh evaluating is the Large/Uncertain/Small technique. The group is being approached to put the things in one of these classes. The initial step is to order the conspicuous things in the two outrageous classifications. Next the gathering can talk about the more mind boggling things. This is really a rearrangements of the basin framework. The framework is particularly great to use in littler gatherings with equivalent things. Next you can appoint sizes to these 3 classifications.

6. Liking Mapping

This technique depends on discovering likenesses in the evaluated things. The group is approached to bunch them. Most ideal path is to execute this is a visual way and request them structure little gatherings to huge. It works best with a little gathering of individuals and a relative modest number of things. You can dole out estimation numbers to the various gatherings. More data about Affinity Mapping.

7. Requesting strategy

This is an activity where you get a precise picture on the overall size of things. This works best in a little gathering of master. All things are put in arbitrary request on a scale mark running from low to high. Each member is being approached to move one thing on the scale. Each move is only one spot lower or one spot higher or pass the turn. This proceeds till no colleague need to move things and passes their turn. The requesting convention is a strategy for getting fine grained size evaluations. Works best with a relative little gathering of individuals and an enormous number of things.

Success stories of those who use Scrum

1. LEGO

Coordinated system utilized: Scaled Agile Framework (SAFe)

Year began: 2015

LEGO started its voyage to dexterity by presenting changes at the group level. There were 20 item groups working at the association at the time. From the start, only 5 groups were changed into self-arranging Scrum groups. At that point, a tiny bit at a time, the staying 15 groups emulated their example.

The consequence of that underlying change was that albeit singular groups had gotten Agile, despite everything they couldn't coordinate viably together. To get that going, LEGO pursued the SAFe system design and included another degree of deliberation - the program level.

At the program level, you have a group of groups (otherwise called Agile Release Train, or ART for short). At LEGO, the group of groups was meeting at regular intervals for a major room arranging session, which went on for one and a half days. During this gathering, groups exhibited their work, worked out the conditions, assessed chances, and made arrangements for the following discharge time frame.

There's likewise the portfolio level, which is the top layer of the framework. This is the place you have long haul field-tested strategies, partners, and top administration. Such division into hierarchical levels is run of the mill for the SAFe system.

LEGO scaling light-footed examination

Results

When you've engaged engineers to deal with their own work, bid farewell to the military of "directors with spreadsheets." You can quit doing inordinate documentation and other ineffective practices.

Engineers currently give progressively exact evaluations, and the results have gotten increasingly unsurprising. Already, the individual who yelled the most intense could complete their work quicker. Presently, with perceivability taken to the extraordinary, choices depend on genuine need.

Nothing beats vis-à-vis correspondence and the beneficial outcome it has on camaraderie. Particularly the correspondence that happens during LEGO's huge room occasions.

LEGO scaling light-footed investigation

Visual, nearly gamified arranging helps center, makes things clear and simpler to determine. Giving individuals autonomy additionally makes them increasingly spurred, and they improve work.

2. Cisco

Lithe system utilized: Scaled Agile Framework (SAFe)

Year began: 2015

This contextual analysis has been composed by Cisco's Ashish Pandey. If it's not too much trouble note that it concerns a particular Cisco item - the Subscription Billing Platform.

The task used to pursue the Waterfall approach. Cisco used to have separate center groups answerable for configuration, fabricate, test, and convey. Deformities were many, and cutoff times were by and large every now and again missed. Individuals were staying at work past 40 hours.

When they changed to SAFe in 2015, this is what occurred.

Cisco made three ARTs* (Agile Release Trains) for:

- Capabilities

- Defects/fixes

- Projects

*In the SAFe system, an ART (Agile Release Train) is basically a group of groups.

Cisco voyage to nimbleness

Consistently, the group had a 15-minute gathering to decide work things. With SAFe, they achieved more noteworthy straightforwardness: each group realized what different groups were doing and groups had the option to oversee themselves, advancing responsibility through notices/mindfulness.

They likewise joined it with the Scrum structure that was being utilized on another item - the WebEx application for Samsung. Some XP rehearses, for example, test-driven advancement and persistent reconciliation (CI), were utilized, as well. The end is that you can utilize one structure for one item and another Agile system for another inside a similar association.

Results

When Cisco began following the SAFe technique, began to discharge regularly, and presented Continuous Integration (CI), they got:

A 40% abatement in basic and significant imperfections.

A 16% diminishing in DRR (Defect Rejected Ratio).

A 14% improvement in DRE (Defect Removal Efficiency) - because of CI and more collaboration between global groups.

There is no more extra time, and the item addition is conveyed on schedule.

3. Lithe Delivery at British Telecom

Lithe structure utilized: Scrum + XP; 90-day conveyance cycles

Year began: 2004

This is a contextual analysis by Ian Evans of British Telecom that discussions about the organization's change to Agile. In 2004, another CIO landed at British Telecom and chose to change the Waterfall procedure. The old model was causing various issues:

- Too numerous individuals were producing prerequisites; practically all necessities had a high need; endeavors were made to crush a greatest number of work things into the following discharge.

- There were such a large number of delegates during the structure organize and an agonizing endorsement process.

- Development cutoff times were difficult to meet; there was a ton of weight on the engineers and brief period for QA.

- Deployment was a bad dream. A few discharges or even whole projects were disposed of as being "past the point where it is possible to the gathering," being never again monetarily suitable or excessively surrey.

To take care of these issues, British Telecom chose to embrace an Agile way to deal with programming improvement and change to shorter discharge cycles:

- Instead of archiving all necessities in advance, they chose do client stories and ceaseless conveyance.

- Customers ought to be straightforwardly included to encourage endorsements and guarantee everybody is in agreement.

- They began doing littler, progressively visit emphasess to improve quality and possess more energy for incorporating additions into the entirety.

English Telecom scaling Agile

Results

At the point when two years went since the change, nobody at British Telecom was happy to return to the old Waterfall model.

These were a portion of the accomplishments:

The conveyance cycle went from a year to 90 days. It currently begins with a three-day broad gathering, at which investors are additionally present.

Everybody included has consented to set severe needs and spotlight just on stories that drive business esteem.

Toward the finish of each cycle, the program is assessed against a lot of accomplishment markers. The group might be paid a reward contingent upon the outcomes.

Accomplishing things the Agile way has improved designer confidence and inspiration.

4. The National Bank of Canada

Nimble system utilized: Scrum of Scrums

Year began: 2012

This contextual investigation discusses the National Bank of Canada's reception of Agile. One of the key difficulties for them was to adjust consistence prerequisites and Agile practices to accomplish as a lot of nimbleness as they could. There were unquestionably tradeoffs to be made. There were numerous things that NBoC just couldn't leave to risk.

Results

To accommodate the requirement for deftness and the need of satisfying certain consistence needs, NBoC landed at some "center ground" choices:

Excess prerequisites ought to get closed down before they can be chosen for a Sprint.

Dash endorsements were presented.

It was chosen to make a long haul Sprint guide that mirrored the organization's key plans.

Engineering was made a deliverable, and it should have been settled on right off the bat in the venture (while Agile by and large encourages you to make significant duties as late as would be prudent.)

Additionally, since they were intensely controlled, the NBoC landed at an intriguing, creative technique for getting a 2-month Spring endorsed. They consider it the - 30 (short thirty) plan. As indicated by this arrangement, a group begins assembling and getting endorsements for future work things in the present dash (30 days ahead of time, consequently the - 30 name.)

All things considered, the change brought about four significant advancements:

Scrum of scrums contextual investigation

5. PTC

Nimble system utilized: Disciplined Agile Delivery (DAD)

Year began: 2014

This contextual investigation discusses Dave Dame helping PTC achieve dexterity by following the DAD (Disciplined Agile Delivery) approach. This technique is intended for organizations that have:

- Large groups

- Distributed groups

- Legacy code (as per insights, about 90% of all Agile group are managing inheritance code)

- A ton of intricacy, authoritative and something else (for example specialized unpredictability)

- Regulatory consistence

These were valid for Dave's situation. Before he took on PTC's case, he got them to recognize that Agile was not a silver projectile and couldn't be depended on to take care of the entirety of their issues.

The difficulties

From various perspectives, PTC was confronting indistinguishable difficulties from the National Bank of Canada from the past contextual investigation:

It was a vigorously directed space, with a great deal of administrative consistence required.

To start with, they'd generally have holes between dashes since it was requiring some investment to concede to work things and get them endorsed.

At first, they typically had "overflow" - incomplete work from a past dash that should have been persisted.

It was hard for designers and directors to concur on a typical Definition of Done. Groups needed their own DoD, yet more often than not it was dubious to accommodate it with the venture wide standard.

The outcomes

What they did at PTC to take care of the four above-depicted issues:

To abstain from getting endorsement for each minor component, Dave chose to separate between high-hazard and okay stories. Generally safe stories don't require endorsements, and groups can make sense of them all alone.

From the start, a group would complete a run and would hold up until they could begin the following one. To address that, PTC made an Elaboration group. The's group will probably ceaselessly take a shot at social occasion highlights from clients/investors. They might be draftsmen or salesmen. This killed delays between dashes.

To anticipate work overflow, PTC figured they expected to improve arranging and prepping. They additionally put aside time in each change and included handling specialized obligation into the arranged work.

It was chosen to have 2 degrees of DoD, where each group would have its DoD, yet additionally there would be an extensive DoD to help keep up a typical quality.

Scrum of scrums contextual investigation

In Conclusion

We should attempt to single out what the above contextual analyses share for all intents and purpose. These organizations that executed scaled Agile structures watched

Scrum and extreme programming (XP)

Scrum and Extreme Programming (XP) are unquestionably adjusted. Actually, in the event that you strolled in a group doing one of these procedures you may have hard time rapidly choosing whether you had strolled in on a Scrum group or a XP group. The distinctions are regularly very inconspicuous, however they are significant. I think there are four primary contrasts among Scrum and XP:

Scrum groups regularly work in cycles (called dashes) that are from about fourteen days to one month long. XP groups commonly work in cycles that are half a month long.

Scrum groups don't permit changes into their runs. When the dash arranging meeting is finished and a dedication made to conveying a lot of item accumulation things, that arrangement of things stays unaltered through the finish of the run. XP groups are substantially more agreeable to change inside their cycles. For whatever length of time that the group hasn't began deal with a specific component, another element of equal size can be swapped into the XP group's emphasis in return for the unstarted include.

Outrageous Programming groups work in a severe need request. Highlights to created are organized by the client (Scrum's Product Owner) and the group is required to chip away at them in a specific order. Conversely, the Scrum item proprietor organizes the item excess yet the group decides the succession where they will build up the build-up things. I've never observed a Scrum group not decide to chip away at the most elevated need thing. Furthermore, a Scrum group will probably decide to deal with the second generally significant. Nonetheless, sooner or later one of the high need things may not be a solid match for the dash being arranged— perhaps a key individual who should take a shot at it will be overwhelmed by take a shot at higher need things. Or then again perhaps it bodes well to take a shot at a somewhat lower need thing (suppose #10 on the item build-up rather than #6) on the grounds that the group will work in the code where #10 would be actualized.

Scrum doesn't endorse any designing practices; XP does. I love the XP building rehearses, especially things like test-driven advancement, the emphasis on robotized testing, pair programming, straightforward plan, refactoring, etc. Notwithstanding, I believe it's an error to state to the group "you're self-sorting out, we confide in you, yet you should do these particular building practices...." This sends a blended message to the group that causes perplexity. I love the XP rehearses yet don't care for commanding them. I need groups to find the incentive all alone.

These are little and frequently inconspicuous contrasts among Scrum and XP. In any case, they can profoundly affect the group. My commonplace counsel to groups is "start with Scrum and afterward design your very own rendition of XP." The XP rehearses are magnificent yet they work best and groups focus on them the most stridently in the event that they find them themselves instead of having them ordered. I assist groups with doing this in my training by posing inquiries like, "Would this bug have occurred on the off chance that we'd been doing test-driven advancement?" and "Would we have committed that error on the off chance that we were pairing?"I see genuine XP as a little focus off out there. In the event that a group can go for that and hit the pinpoint center, magnificent. If not, be that as it may, they are likely hacking (e.g., refactoring with no robotized testing or TDD). Scrum is a major dead center that all alone brings enormous upgrades just through the extra concentration and the timeboxed cycles. That is a decent beginning stage for then including the XP rehearses.

Extraordinary Programming (XP) is a deft programming improvement system that expects to create better programming, and higher caliber of life for the advancement group. XP is the most explicit of the deft systems with respect to suitable designing practices for programming improvement.

Scrum is a system inside which individuals can address complex versatile issues, while profitably and imaginatively conveying results of the most noteworthy conceivable worth. Scrum itself is a basic system for powerful group cooperation on complex items.

Scrum and XP are both Agile methodologies that offer the basic ideas of iterative improvement, working programming, discharge and cycle arranging, every day gatherings, review, all components of an Agile procedure. Both approach are adjusted each other that occasionally is hard to recognize a group who is receiving XP while another group who is doing Scrum.

Extraordinary Programming

Extraordinary Programming

Run Cycle

Run Cycle

Best Scrum Software

Best Scrum Software Every Project Needs

An amazing scrum programming that supports scrum venture the executives. It highlights scrum devices like client story map, item build-up the executives, dash excess administration, task the executives, every day scrum meeting, run arranging device, run survey apparatus, run review device, burndown, hindrance, partner and group the executives.

Find out More

There are anyway a few contrasts, some of them extremely inconspicuous, and especially in the accompanying 4 perspectives:

1. Cycle length

Scrum

Regularly from about fourteen days to one month long.

XP

Normally half a month long.

2. Regardless of whether necessities are permitted to be altered in a cycle

Scrum

Try not to permit changes into their dashes.

When the run arranging meeting is finished and a dedication made to convey a lot of item build-up things, that arrangement of things stays unaltered through the finish of the dash.

XP

Significantly more agreeable to change inside their cycles.

For whatever length of time that the group hasn't began chip away at a specific component, another element of proportionate size can be swapped into the XP group's cycle in return for the un-began include.

3. Regardless of whether User Story is actualized carefully as indicated by need in emphasess.

XP

Work in a severe need request.

Highlights to be created are organized by the client (Scrum's Product Owner) and the group is required to deal with them in a specific order.

Scrum

Scrum item proprietor organizes the item build-up yet the group decides the succession where they will build up the excess things.

A Scrum group will probably decide to chip away at the second generally significant.

4. Regardless of whether to embrace exacting building techniques to guarantee progress or quality during the time spent programming execution

Scrum

Doesn't recommend any designing practices;

XP

XP does.

For instance: TDD, pair programming, straightforward structure, refactoring...

We can outline the contrasts among XP and Scrum as pursues:

Aspects	Practices	XP	Scrum

Emphasis Length   Whether to permit adjustment of requirements 1-2   weeks   2 a month

Handle Changes with an Iteration   Whether the interest is carefully as per the priority   It can be supplanted with different necessities when a need isn't executed, however the usage time is equal.   Scrum isn't permitted to do this. When the emphasis is finished, no progressions are permitted, and Scrum Master is carefully checked.

Need of Features   Whether the interest is carefully as per the priority   Yes   No need to

Designing Practices   Whether to embrace exacting building techniques to guarantee progress or quality   Very strict   Require engineers to be cognizant

Along these lines, we accepts that XP's methodology is adequate, however it brings Agile into a befuddling conundrum, on the grounds that the possibility of XP, joined with light-footed mode, passes on to the group the message that "you are a completely self-guided association, yet you need to actualize TDD, pair programming, and so forth."

It isn't hard to find that the four qualifications are very self-evident:

In Scrum, it stresses self-association

In XP, it stresses solid building practice requirements.

How to manage projects with Scrum

We should initially be sure about what Scrum isn't. There is a typical misguided judgment that Agile is Scrum. While Scrum is in reality light-footed, it isn't the underside strategy for actualizing spry standards. Scrum is basically one of numerous deft ways to deal with item improvement. Different techniques incorporate Extreme Programming (XP), Crystal, Feature Driven Development, DSDM Atern, etc. These techniques stick to the Agile Manifesto and its related standards. An accommodating representation is considered Agile being frozen yogurt, while Scrum, XP, Crystal, and so on., are generally basically various flavors, similar to chocolate, strawberry, vanilla. They are altogether lithe, they are on the whole great, and many can be utilized in mix.

Basically, Scrum is a dexterous technique for iterative and gradual item conveyance that utilizations visit criticism and collective basic leadership.

History

Scrum depends on a 1986 paper composed by Hirotaka Takeuchi and Ikujiro Nonaka for the Harvard Business Review titled "The New Product Development Game." In this paper, the creators utilized the game of rugby as a representation to portray the advantages of self-arranging groups in inventive item improvement and conveyance. Jeff Sutherland, Ken Schwaber, and Mike Beedle took the thoughts from this paper, including the illustration, and applied it to their field of programming improvement. They called their new technique Scrum, after the rugby term that portrays how groups structure a circle and go for the ball to get it once more into play once more. They originally applied this strategy at Easel Corporation in 1993. Schwaber and Beedle expounded on their encounters in their book Agile Software Development with Scrum in 2002, trailed by Schwaber's book Agile Project Management with Scrum in 2004, which incorporated the work Schwaber had finished with Primavera.

The Scrum Framework

Schwaber alludes to Scrum as a system and not a technique. This is essentially because of the undertones around the word strategy, which many construe as prescriptive in nature. Conversely, Scrum just gives a structure to conveyance, however doesn't disclose to you how to do explicit works on, leaving that to the group to decide. Display 1 shows the essential Scrum structure.

The Original Scrum Framework

Show 1. The Original Scrum Framework

The venture starts with an unmistakable vision gave by the business, and a lot of item includes arranged by significance. These highlights are a piece of the item excess, which is kept up by the client or client delegate alluded to as the Product Owner. A period box generally alluded to as a cycle or dash, is the set measure of time that the group needs to finish the highlights chose. Dashes are for the most part from one to about a month long, and that length is kept up for the duration of the life of the venture in order to build up a rhythm. The group chooses things from the item excess that it accepts can be finished in the dash, and makes a run accumulation comprising of the highlights and undertakings as a major aspect of the run arranging meeting.

When the group has focused on a dash excess, the assignment work starts. During this time in the dash, the group is shielded from interferences and permitted to concentrate on meeting the run objective.

No progressions to the dash overabundance are permitted; in any case, the item excess can be changed in anticipation of the following run.

During the run, the group checks in day by day with one another as a 15-minute gathering known as a scrum. The group remains around and every part states what they did yesterday, what they intend to do today, and what is holding them up.

Toward the finish of the dash, the group demos the work they have finished to the partners and assembles criticism that will influence what they deal with in the following run. They additionally hold a review to figure out how to improve. This gathering is basic, as its attention is on the three mainstays of Scrum: straightforwardness, review, and adjustment.

Jobs and Responsibilities

There are just three jobs in Scrum: the ScrumMaster, the Product Owner, and the Team.

The ScrumMaster is the attendant of the procedure, the supporter for the group, and the defender of the group. They expel hindrances, encourage group correspondence, intervene exchanges inside the group and consult with those outer to the group. Most importantly, they exist in support of the group.

The Product Owner speaks to the voice of the client and has the power to settle on choices about the item. This individual possesses the item excess and is answerable for imparting the vision to the group, and characterizing and organizing accumulation things. The Product Owner works with the group regularly to respond to questions and give item direction.

The Team comprises of seven give or take two individuals who are mutually answerable for the conveyance of the item. They possess the assessments, make task duties, and report every day status to one another in the day by day scrum. They are self-sorting out, implying that structure shows up without express intercession all things considered. At the end of the day, the group claims how it decides to construct item includes—the group possesses the "how," while the Product Owner possesses the "what."

The Application of Scrum

Scrum is applied by following a lot of functions, or gatherings. Required Scrum services incorporate the run arranging meeting, the everyday scrum, the run survey and the dash review. Working in time boxes called dashes is likewise required. Discharge arranging gatherings are discretionary and take into account the arranging and anticipating of gatherings of dashes.

Dash Planning Meeting

The dash arranging meeting is hung on the primary day of each run. The ScrumMaster, Product Owner, and Team are all in participation. The Product Owner introduces the arrangement of highlights the individual might want to see finished in the run (the "what") at that point the group decides the undertakings expected to execute these highlights (the "how"). Work gauges are checked on to check whether the group has the opportunity to finish every one of the highlights mentioned in the dash. Provided that this is true, the group focuses on the dash. If not, the lower need highlights return into the item overabundance, until the remaining task at hand for the dash is little enough to get the group's dedication.

Following Progress

When the run arranging meeting is finished and the group has made a responsibility, the group starts to keep tabs on its development utilizing profoundly obvious data radiators. These radiators incorporate the burndown graph and the assignment board.

The assignment board is utilized by the group to follow the advancement of the errands for each component. The base sections utilized are To Do, Doing, and Done. Groups will have their day by day scrum meeting at the errand board, and move things no matter how you look at it while expressing what they did yesterday, what they intend to do today, and what snags they are pondering. See Exhibit 2 for a model errand board for a product improvement venture.

Scrum Task Board Example (Graphic politeness of Mountain Goat Software. All rights saved.)

The burndown outline shows the pattern line of the measure of work left to do in the dash. The x-pivot is the quantity of days in the run, and the y-hub is the quantity of hours for every one of the assignments that were characterized in the run arranging meeting. Throughout the times of the run, the line showing the measure of work left to do should drift down to zero by the most recent day of the run. See Exhibit 3 for a run burndown outline model.

Run Burndown Chart Example

Display 3. Run Burndown Chart Example

Run progress is followed utilizing the burndown outline, the undertaking board, and the day by day scrum. In blend, these three things can give an unmistakable image of what's being dealt with, what's finished, what's still to be done, regardless of whether it will be finished in time, and what may be keeping the group from meeting its dash and additionally discharge objective.

Run Review

Toward the finish of the run, the group welcomes partners to a dash survey meeting where the highlights that were finished in the run are demo'd and input is mentioned. The Product Owner monitors the criticism and consolidates it as required into the item build-up.

When the audit is finished, the group (without the partners) leads a review to figure out what they did well that they wish to keep doing, what they battled with, and what proposals they have for change going ahead. An activity plan is made and these things are actualized throughout the following dash, and surveyed for adequacy in the following run review.

Discharge Planning

Discharge Planning is additionally part of Scrum, and is an approach to do long haul getting ready for a period box that comprises of numerous runs. This is frequently done quarterly, and the consequences of the quarter don't need to be a discharge to the client, yet may basically be an inward discharge to affirm framework coordination and approval. Display 4 shows how discharge arranging fits in with the remainder of the Scrum structure.

The whole group goes to the discharge arranging meeting, where the Product Owner shows the highlights, she/he might want to see finished in the quarter. The group doesn't task out these highlights be that as it may, however rather gives net level assessments to figure out what highlights should be possible in what dash, and what number of these highlights can be finished before the finish of the quarter. Discharge arranging can be highlight driven (what number of runs will it take to finish this arrangement of highlights?), time-driven (what number of highlights would we be able to hope to have finished by this cutoff time?) or cost-driven (given this spending limit, what does our timetable resemble and what highlights will we have done before we come up short on cash?

Tips for Scrum mastery

1. Be a worker chief

The worker chief is hireling first. Concentrate on the development and prosperity of your colleagues. Help your colleagues and evacuate hindrances. Put their needs first to ensure each colleague can execute as exceptionally as could reasonably be expected.

2. Concentrate on each undertaking in turn

You might be fit for dealing with different ventures, however this could likewise imply that you're mostly dedicated to an undertaking. To give your full 100% and to ensure the undertaking is as effective as it tends to be, handle each task in turn.

3. Help the group characterize a reasonable meaning of done

Ensure the meaning of done is unmistakably characterized. It ought to be a rundown containing all things that must be finished to convey a quality programming. Help the group to characterize quality checks, with the goal that a colleague realizes how to decide whether an assignment is done true to form.

4. Continue learning and exploring

The world is evolving. Ensure you change with it. In the event that you don't, it implies that you're moving in reverse rather than forward! As a scrum ace, it's your duty to ensure your group advances and continues improving at their work and cooperation. You can't do this without learning and improving your aptitudes and information. Help your group develop by developing yourself.

5. Know your group

Ensure you know each colleague. What are their qualities and shortcomings? What are their characters? Do you know the group's dynamic? Would you be able to name the life partner and diversions? Attempt to find out about your colleagues. On the off chance that you realize them well, you'll figure out how to assist them with functioning better together.

6. Try not to appear for the every day stay standing for a couple of days

As a scrum ace, it is your objective to make a self-arranging group. To arrive at this objective, urge the group to give updates and input to one another rather than to you. You may attempt to do this by not appearing for the day by day stand up a couple of days, this will offer the group the chance to self-encourage.

7. Convey, impart, convey

The achievement of a scrum venture relies upon clear and continuous correspondence in the group. As a scrum ace, it is your activity that the improvement group, item proprietor and partners are forward-thinking constantly. Ensure objectives and undertakings are clear for everybody and that they are refreshed consistently.

8. Ensure the group is associated with ceaseless improvement

During the review, the group attempts to discover approaches to improve the procedure, in view of their encounters in the dash. Ensure you propel everybody to ponder the procedure and to continue considering in during the entire procedure.

This is significant for the group to continue improving.

9. Inquire as to whether what you're doing is in accordance with the Agile standards

As a scrum ace, you are answerable for ensuring the whole group effectively adheres to the standards and standards of Scrum. You're the person who mentors the group every single Agile practice. Along these lines, occasionally, return to the Agile standards and guarantee that what you are doing is in accordance with every one of them.

Scrum mistakes to avoid

1. Anticipating that Transformation should Agile and Scrum to Be Easy

Very regularly, somebody will get a book on Agile or Scrum, start cleaving up prerequisites into client stories, start every day stand-up gatherings, create programming in 2-multi week runs, and afterward call themselves Agile. Simple, correct? They will probably observe some improvement in their capacity to react to change, and may even give working programming quicker – to some time. It won't be excessively long, however, until the guarantees of Agile become less obvious, groups battle to keep up the pace, programming doesn't generally coordinate client desires, and afterward Agile is regarded a disappointment. Nimble change requires some serious energy and quite often begins muddled. Genuine change uncovered existing corporate and culture issues that must be managed – issues, for example, poor correspondence, absence of responsibility, doubt, and so on. Successful Agile change is regularly an absolute culture change. Give it time, and be all set through the torment and protection from social changes.

2. Doing the Practices Without the Principles

Accomplishing the simple things like actualizing Scrum gatherings, filling the Scrum jobs, and utilizing appropriate Scrum antiques is great, however is just half (or less) of the fight. The Agile standards are what make the practices function admirably, and make them reasonable over the long haul. Standards are a lot harder to consolidate than rehearses, which is the reason numerous organizations miss the mark — they don't do the hard parts. Utilizing procedures without understanding why you are doing them can prompt disappointment. Lithe is about individuals, collaborations, and culture, not procedures, practices, and apparatuses.

3. Muddling the Agile/Scrum Startup

Do all that you can to keep Agile new companies straightforward. Nimble tasks can be fruitful without the most recent, coolest coordinated effort or lifecycle instrument. Stickies on a divider, assignments in a spreadsheet, and a physically created torch diagram will take care of business. Investing important energy getting an instrument going as opposed to getting individuals cooperating is concentrating on an inappropriate thing. The Agile Manifesto places higher incentive on people and communications than on procedures and devices.

4. Driving a Scrum Team Like a Project Manager

A "direction and control" mindset is counter to the Agile system. A pioneer allocating undertakings and managing exertion is an Agile enemy of example. Extraordinary Agile groups are self-sorting out, the Scrum Master is a hireling chief, and groups figure out how to turn out to be better at cooperating and conveying more prominent worth all the more proficiently by normal investigation and adaption. Regularly the exercise is found out better by understanding (fortunate or unfortunate experience) than by simply being determined what to do. Permit the Scrum group to make sense of things for themselves, to commit errors and gain from them, and to accomplish the fulfillment of turning into a beneficial group without anyone else. Scrum Masters and Agile mentors control more than they drive.

5. An Un-Ready Product Backlog

An item accumulation that isn't "prepared" is one of the most widely recognized explanations behind run disappointment and for unmotivated groups. It is likewise a main driver for low conveyance speed and not conveying high worth. Most new Product Owners aren't prepared to be profitable all alone. They need guidance, instructing, and hand-holding for the initial scarcely any dashes as they figure out how to create and keep up an item build-up that has enough important highlights assessed at a significant level, and organized by business esteem. Setting up the accumulation well in front of the following sprint(s) is an absolute necessity. You never need the group to come up short on work to do, and that work must be of most noteworthy incentive by then as organized by the Product Owner. Being a Product Owner can be tedious. Set the correct desires, give all the preparation, and help the Product Owner to keep the progression of significant worth coming.

6. Imparting "Through" the Scrum Master

Something I see normally on new Scrum groups is individuals utilizing the Scrum Master to convey their messages to other people. For instance, an engineer has an inquiry concerning a client story; rather than going straightforwardly to the Product Owner, he/she messages the Scrum Master to get the data. A key Agile rule is conveying up close and personal at whatever point conceivable. The time it takes to make the email would almost certainly have been every one of that was expected to find the solution legitimately from the partner. Be that as it may, for some, specialized individuals, up close and personal correspondence is a startling thing when they're accustomed to living in their work space world, without conversing with individuals. This is a social or character issue that must be survived. It sits around idly and, all the more significantly, expands the danger of miscommunication.

7. A Product Owner Who isn't Available Or Involved

The Product Owner job can be very tedious. Numerous who are new to the job are not prepared for the responsibility, or simply don't have a clue about that they should be so included. Cooperation is basic in the Agile world. Businessmen and engineers need to cooperate to deliver programming that the business needs. This occurs by steady correspondence, coordinated effort and short input cycles to approve or make course revisions. A training I love to see is the Product Owner so engaged with the everyday action of the task group that the Sprint Review is absolutely a convention in light of the fact that the Product Owner has just observed a few cycles of the highlights all through the run and has guided the group to manufacture precisely what the business needs. That is an excellent thing.

8. Careless Daily Stand-ups

The day by day stand-up meeting is significant from a few angles. It puts individuals eye to eye each day for 15 minutes, powers correspondence and joint effort, and gives perceivability and straightforwardness into the task. For such a key gathering, it's essential to set the correct desires in advance so the group pays attention to it. This may sound activist, yet participation at the day by day stand-up is rarely discretionary. Start on schedule and complete on schedule. Adhere to the three inquiries (what did I achieve for the task yesterday, what will I chip away at today, what impediments are blocking me from finishing my work on schedule). Try not to permit side discussions, talks, or critical thinking during the stand-up; those should all be possible after the stand-up is done. This gets the group in the method of regarding the group and individuals' time, and they figure out how to convey better by adhering to the targets and being brief.

9. Not Raising Obstacles Early Enough

The day by day stand-up gives the open door consistently to convey obstacles to completing our work. One of the essential elements of the Scrum Master is to expel snags so the group can concentrate on conveying programming; however in the event that hindrances are not raised, the Scrum Master can't help evacuate them. Standing by to raise an impediment until it's past the point where it is possible to recuperate from it is unsatisfactory. Until colleagues are familiar with imparting deterrents in an opportune way, remind the group toward the start of each rise up to raise even potential snags, or if there's any opportunity something may defer their work or prompt them to not satisfy their dash responsibility.

10. Not Conducting Retrospective Meetings After Every Sprint

One of the twelve standards behind the Agile Manifesto is "At ordinary interims, the group considers how to turn out to be progressively compelling, at that point tunes and modifies its conduct in like manner". Lamentably the Sprint Retrospective is frequently treated like an extra or an extravagance, and performed just "if there's time". The truth of the matter is, Agile is about alterations to a great extent, calibrating and reacting to change. It's extremely difficult to alter and calibrate on the off chance that we don't delay to discover where modifications are required. Business as usual isn't Agile; persistent improvement is.

Conclusion

An opportunity to showcase programming items have been abbreviated exponentially in the present aggressive worldwide situation. The item life cycle or framework improvement starts from statistical surveying of an idea or the need of a customer and finishes in framework arrangements and activity. The worldwide challenge and change in client's need have brought about scrum proclamation, which is required to quickly build up a framework and to meet change in necessities started by the client even late in the improvement arrange. Proof shows that scrum has picked up ubiquity and will proceed in the numerous years to come. While there are numerous hindrances of utilizing customary philosophy on ventures.